Robert Williams Buchanan

The Buchanan Ballads

Old and new

Robert Williams Buchanan

The Buchanan Ballads
Old and new

ISBN/EAN: 9783744796729

Printed in Europe, USA, Canada, Australia, Japan

Cover: Foto ©Thomas Meinert / pixelio.de

More available books at **www.hansebooks.com**

THE

BUCHANAN BALLADS,

Old and New.

BY

ROBERT BUCHANAN.

Clown. What hast here? Ballads?
Mopsa. Pray now, buy some; I love a ballad in print o' life,
    for then we are sure they are true.'
Autolycus. Here's one to a very doleful tune.
Mopsa. Is it true, think you?
Autolycus. Very true, and but a month old . . . This is a
    merry ballad, but a very pretty one.
Mopsa. Let's have some merry ones."
                —THE WINTER'S TALE.

London:

JOHN HADDON & CO., SALISBURY SQUARE, E.C.,

AND ALL BOOKSELLERS.

1892.

PREFATORY NOTE.

OF the poems which follow, a few are already familiar to the great public, while some are entirely new, and now published for the first time. Such pieces as the " Wake of O'Hara," "Shon Maclean," "Phil Blood's Leap" and "Fra Giacomo" have long been used for purposes of public recitation.

In the poem called "Hallelujah Jane" an attempt is made to do justice to the nobler side of the great social Crusade led by "General" Booth, a Crusade which, despite some disagreeable features and a barbarous terminology, has awakened the sleeping conscience of the world to the sufferings of countless human beings. I have gone to the life for my picture, and have omitted no detail on either sentimental or prudish grounds. In the Ode addressed to the Empress Victoria, and published originally in the *Contemporary Review*, no note of mere flattery was sounded, but occasion was taken to point out those blots which still disfigure our boasted civilization; so that, in one respect at least, the Ode had an unique purpose. The lines on "the Burial of Parnell" (supposed to be spoken by one of his personal followers) are without any sort of moral or political bias. The business of a poet is to utter the truth dramatically, and fearlessly as well as clearly; this I have tried to do, at the risk of any kind of misconstruction.

I desire in these prefatory words to chronicle the courage and the generosity of the first man who, at a moment when the intellectual Scribes and Pharisees hung back, gave a practical answer to General Booth's great Appeal, and I do so with the more pleasure because this man belongs to a profession with which Puritanism has never shown any sympathy. I know of no more large-minded conception of true philanthropy than that expressed, on the occasion in question, by Mr. S. B. BANCROFT, to whom, with all sincere respect, I dedicate these " Ballads."

ROBERT BUCHANAN.

Dec. 3, 1891.

CONTENTS.

THE BUCHANAN BALLADS.

"STORM IN THE NIGHT."

STORM in the Night, Buchanan! a Voice in the night
  still crying,
" They have taken away my Lord, and I know not where
  he is lying! "

Thou, too, singer of songs and dreamer of dreams, art
  weeping
For the Form that lay in the tomb, the Face so peacefully
  sleeping ;

And now he hath gone indeed, and his worshippers roam
  bereaven,
Thou, by the Magdalen's side, art standing and looking at
  Heaven!

Woe unto thee, Buchanan! and woe to thy generation!
The harp of the heart he strung, the Soul he set in
  vibration,

Are lost since he is lost, the beautiful Elder Brother ;
For the harp of the heart was his, the song could gladden
  no other!

'Twas something,—nay, 'twas much!—to know, though
  his life was over,
That the fair, bright Form was there, with the wool-white
  shroud for a cover !

7

He did not speak or stir, he did not hark to our weeping,
But his grave grew wide as the World, and the stars
smiled down on his sleeping.

He made no speech, no sign, for Death has disrobed and
discrown'd him,—
But the scent of spikenard and myrrh was sweet in the
air around him !

So we kept our Brother, tho' dead !   The Lily Flower of
Creation !
And to touch his dear dead hands was joy in our deso-
lation.

But *now*, the Tomb is void, and the rain beats over the
portal :
Thieves like wolves in the night have stolen the dead
Immortal !

So peacefully he slept, the Lily Flower of Creation,
That we said to ourselves, "He dreams ! and his dream
is the World's salvation ! "

But now by the Tomb we stand, despairing and heavy-
hearted :
The stars look silently down, but the Light of the World
hath departed.

And yet, should he be risen ?   Should he have waken'd,
to wander
Out 'mid the winds of the night, out 'mid the Tempest
yonder,

Holding his Lamp wind-blown, while the rain-cloud
darkens and gathers,
Feeling his way thro' the gloom, naming our names, and
our Father's ?

Nay, for the World would know the face of the fair New
    Comer,
The graves would open wide, like buds at the breath of
    the summer,—

The graves would open, the Dead within them quicken
    and blossom,
And over the World would rain the flowers that had
    grown in his bosom !

Nay, then, he hath fled, not risen ! in vain we seek and
    implore him !
Deeper than Death he hath fall'n, and the waves of the
    World roll o'er him !

Storm in the night, Buchanan ! A Voice in the night still
    crying,
" They have taken away our Lord ! and we know not
    where he is lying ! "

THE BALLAD OF THE MAGDALEN.

I saw on the Bridge of Sorrow, when all the City
   slept,
The shape of a woeful Woman, who look'd at Heaven,
   and wept.

Loose o'er her naked shoulders trembled her night-black
   hair;
Her robe was ragged and rent, and her feet were bleeding
   and bare.

And, lo! in her hands she carried a vessel with spices
   sweet,
And she cried, "Where art thou, Master? I come to
   anoint thy feet."

Then I touch'd her on the shoulder: "What thing art
   thou?" I said;
And she stood and gazed upon me with eyes like the eyes
   of the dead.

But I saw the painted colour flash on her cheeks and
   lips,
While she stood and felt in the vessel with tremulous
   finger-tips.

And she answer'd never a word, but stood in the lonely
   light,
With the evil of earth upon her, and the darkness of
   Death and Night.

And I knew her then by her beauty, her sin and the sign
  of her shame,
And touch'd her again more gently, and sadly named her
  name.

She heard, and she did not answer; but her tears began
  to fall,
And again, " Where art thou, Master?" I heard her thin
  voice call.

And she would have straightway left me, but I held her
  fast and said,
While the chill wind moan'd around us, and the stars
  wept overhead,

" O Mary, where is thy Master? Where does he hide
  his face?
The world awaits his coming, but knows not the time or
  the place.

" O Mary, lead me to him—He loved thee deep and
  true;
Since thou hast risen to find him, he must be risen
  too."

Then the painted lips made answer, while the dead eyes
  gazed on me :
" I have sought him all through the Cities, and yonder
  in Galilee.

" I have sought him and not found him, I have search'd
  in every land,
Though the door of the Tomb was open, and the shroud
  lay shrunk in the sand.

" Long through the years I waited, there in the shade of
    the tomb,
Then I rose and went to meet him, out in the World's
    great gloom.

" And I took pollution with me, wherever my footsteps
    came ;
Yes, I shook my sin on the Cities, my sin and the sign of
    my shame.

" Yet I knew if I could find him, and kneel and anoint
    his feet,
That his gentle hands would bless me, and our eyes at
    last would meet.

" And my sin would fall and leave me, and peace would
    fill my breast,
And there, in the Tomb he rose from, I could lie me down
    and rest."

Tall in the moonlit City, pale as some statue of stone,
With the evil of earth upon her, she stood and she made
    her moan.

And away on the lonely bridges, and under the gaslight
    gleam,
The pale street-walker heard her, a voice like a voice in a
    dream.

For, lo! in her hands she carried a vessel with spices
    sweet,
And she cried, " Where art thou, Master ? I come to
    anoint thy feet."

Then my living force fell from me, and I stood and
    watch'd her go
From shrine to shrine in the starlight, with feeble feet
    and slow.

And the stars look'd down in sorrow, and the earth lay
 black beneath,
And the sleeping City was cover'd with shadows of night
 and death,

While I heard the faint voice wailing afar in the stony
 street,
" Where art thou, Master, Master ? I come to anoint
 thy feet."

"HALLELUJAH JANE."

" He's a long way off, is Jesus—and we've *got* to make it loud!"

Glory! Hallelujah! March along together!
March along, march along, every kind of weather!
Wet or dry, shower or shine, ready night and day,
Travelling to Jesus, singing on the way!
He is waiting for us, yonder in the sky,
Stooping down His shining head to
                                    Hear
                                            Our
                                                    Cry!

"'Alleloojah! 'alleloojah! Round the corner of the
    street,
They're a-coming and a-singing, with a sound of tramping
    feet.
Throw the windy open, Jenny—let me 'ear the fife and
    drum—
Garn! the cold can't 'arm *me*, Jenny—ain't I book'd for
    Kingdom Come?
I've got the doctor's ticket for a third-class seat, ye know,
And the Lord 'll blow his whistle, and the train begin to
    go.
Alleloojah! How I love 'em!—and the music—and the
    rhyme—
My 'eart's a-marchin' with 'em, and my feet is beatin'
    time!
Lift me up, and let me see them—Lord, how bright they
    looks to-day!
Ain't it 'eavenly? Men and women, boys and gels, they
    march away!

Who's that wavin'? It's the Captain, bless his 'art! He
    sees me plain—
It was 'im as 'ad me chris'en'd, call'd me ' 'Alleloojah
    Jane!'
And the minute I was chris'en'd, somethink lep' in my
    inside,
And I saw, fur off and shining, Golden Gates as open'd
    wide,
And I 'eard the Angels 'oller, and I answered loud and
    clear,
And the blessèd, larfing Jesus cried, ' You've got to march
    up 'ere!'
And I march'd and lep' and shouted till my throat was
    sick and sore,
Down I tumbled with diptheery, and I couldn't march no
    more!"

Glory! Hallelujah! Sound the fife and drum!
Brother, won't you join us, bound for Kingdom Come?
Wear our regimentals, spick and span and gay,
And be always ready to listen and obey?
Form in marching order, stepping right along,
While above the angels smile and
                Join
                  Our
                    Song?

"Are they gone? Well, lay me down, Jenny—for p'r'aps
    this very day
The Lord 'll read the roll-call, so there ain't much time
    to stay.
But afore I leave yer, Jenny, for the trip as all must take,
Jest you 'ear me bless the music that fust blew my soul
    awake.

I was born in dirt and darkness—I was blind and dumb
  with sin—
For the typhus 'ad took father, and my mother's-milk
  was gin,
And at sixteen I was walkin' like the other gels ye meet,
And I kep' a little sister by my earnin's on the street.
Well, they say 'twas orful sinful, but 'twas all I'd got to
  do,
For I 'ad to get my livin', and to keep my sister too;
And poor Bess, yer see, was sickly—for she'd never been
  the same
Since she got a kick from father on the back, wot made
  her lame ;—
As for mother, she was berried too, thank God! One
  winter night
Been run over by a Pickford, when mad drunk, and serve
  her right !
So we two was left together, and poor Bess, 'twas 'ard for
  'er,
For her legs was thin as matches, and she couldn't scursly
  stir ;
But so pretty ! with her thin face, and her silken yeller
  'air,
And so 'andy with her needle, in her invalidy chair.
And when at night I left her to walk out in street and
  lane,
Tho' I come 'ome empty-'anded, she'd a kiss for sister
  Jane.
But 'twas 'ard, and allays 'arder, just to keep ourselves at
  all,
Me so precious black and ugly, Bess so 'flicted and so
  small,
For tho' only one year younger, she'd 'a past for twelve
  or less ;
But, Lor bless ye, she was clever, and could read and
  spell, could Bess !

(She'd learnt it at the 'ospital from some kind nuss, yer
see.)
When I brought 'er 'ome a paper she could read the noos
to me,
All the p'lice noos and the murders, and the other rum
things there,
And for 'ours I'd sit and listen, by her invalidy chair!

Well, one night as I was climbin' up the stair, tired out
and sad,
For the luck had been ag'in me, and 'twas pourin' down
like mad,
I 'eard her voice a-screaming! and from floor to floor I
ran,
Till I reach'd our room and sor 'er, and beside her was a
man,
An ugly Spanish sailor as was lodgin' in the place,
And the beast was 'olding Bessie and a-kissing of her face,
And she cried and scream'd and struggled, a-tryin' to get
free,
And the beast he 'eard me comin' and turned round 'is
face to me,
And I sor it black and ugly with the drink and worse
beside,
And I screech'd, 'Let go my sister!' while she 'id her
face and cried.
Then the man look'd black as thunder, and he swore he'd
'ave my life
If I stay'd there, and his fingers began feelin' for his knife,
But I lep' and seized a poker as was lying by the grate,
And I struck 'im on the forrid (bet your life he got it
straight—
For I felt as strong as twenty!), and he guv an angry
groan,
Drew the knife, and lep' to stab me, then roll'd over like
a stone!

B

And the landlord and the lodgers came a-rushin' up the
    stair,
While I knelt by Bess, who'd fainted in her invalidy chair!

Well, Jenny, no one blamed me!—and the p'lice said
    ' Serve him right!'—
I never saw his face ag'in arter that drefful night;
But ever arter that poor Bess seem'd dull and full of care,
And she droop'd and droop'd and sicken'd in her invalidy
    chair.
Some trouble of the 'art, they said (that shock was her
    death-blow!)
And I watched her late and early, and I knew as she
    must go ;
And the doctor gave her physic, and she'd all as she could
    eat,
And I bought her many a relish, when I'd luck upon the
    street ;
But one mornin', close on Easter, when I waken'd in our
    bed,
I turn'd and see her lyin' with her arms out, stiff and
    dead !
And I cried a bit and kiss'd her, then got out o' bed and
    drest,
Wash'd her face, put on clean linen, placed her 'ands upon
    her breast,
And she look'd . . . she look'd . . . *so* pretty !
        God was good ! I'd luck just then—
I scraped the money somehow, till I'd nigh on one pound
    ten,
And I bought poor Bess a coffin, and a grave where she
    could lie
She got no workus berryin'—thank God for *that*, sez I !
And the neighbours sor me foller, all a-gatherin' in a
    crowd,
And I never felt as lonesome, but I never felt so proud !

Arter that, I sort o' drifted 'ere and there about the town,
Like a smut blown from a chimbly, and a long time
   comin' down!
And I took to drink like mother, and the drink it made
   me mad,
So, between the streets and prison, well, my luck was
   orful bad!
I was 'onest, tho', and never robb'd a man, or thief'd (not
   me!)
Tho' they quodded me for fightin', and bad langwidge,
   don't yer see?
And at last, somehow or other, how it come about ain't
   clear,
I was took to the Lock 'Ospital, and kep' there nigh a
   year.
And I felt—well, now, I'll tell yer—like a bit of orange
   peel,
All muddy and all rotten, wot you squash beneath your
   'eel.
Well, the doctors 'eal'd and cured me, but one mornin,'
   when they said,
I might go to a reformat'ry, sez I, 'No, strike me dead!'
And I felt a kind o' loathin' for them all, and thought
   of Bess
Lyin' peaceful there at Stepney in her clean white fun'ral
   dress.
And I left the Lock next mornin'—I was wild, ye see,
   to go—
And 'twas Christmas, when I trampled back to Stepney
   thro' the snow—
And I met a chap who treated me and made me blazin'
   tight,
And I lost my 'ed and waken'd in the streets at dead
   o' night,
And the snow was fallin', fallin', and 'twas thick upon
   the ground,

And I'd got no place to go to, and my 'ed was whirlin'
round,
When I see a lamp afore me, and a door stood open wide,
And I took it for a publick, till they sang a psalm inside,
And I sez, ' It's them Salvationists! ' and turned to go
away,
When one comes out, their Captain, and calls out for me
to stay ;
And he touch'd me on the shoulder, and he sez, ' Wot's
up, my lass ? '
And I sez, ' *I* ain't teatotal! ' and I larf'd, and tried to
pass,
But he look'd me in the face, he did, and sez, ' Wot
brings ye 'ere?
Speak out, if you're in trouble, and we'll 'elp ye, never
fear! '
And I sez. ' I *ain't* in trouble! ' but he looks me in the
eyes.
And he answers sharp and sudden, ' Don't you tell me
any *lies*—
The Lord Jesus 'ates a liar! ' and at that I shut my fist,
I'd 'a struck 'im if 'ed let me, but he ketch'd me by the
wrist,
And he whisper'd, oh, so gentle, ' You're our sister, lass,'
he said,
' And to-night I think our sister 'as no place to lay her
'ed !
Come in — your friends are waitin' — they've been
waitin' many a day —
And at last you've come, my sister, and I think you've
come to stay! ' "

Glory ! Hallelujah ! Fighting for the Lord !
Sinners kneel before us, fearing fire and sword !
Never you take service with the Devil's crew —
Here you'll get promotion, if you're straight and true !

Jesus is Field-Marshal, Jesus, Heaven's King,
Points us forward, forward, while we
>*March*
>>*And*
>>>*Sing!*

"Still a-playin' in the distance! 'Alleloojah! Fife and
drum!
'Ere's my blessin' on the music, now I'm bound for
Kingdom Come!
Well, that night?—They guv me shelter, and a shake-
down nice and clean,
And no one ax'd no questions—who I was, or wot I'd
been—
But next mornin' when I wakened, with a 'ed that split
in two,
In there comes a nice old lady, and sez smilin', 'How d'ye
do?'
And I nods and answers sulky, for 'she's come to preach,'
thinks I,
But we gets in conversation, and at last, the Lord knows
why,
I tells her about Bessie,—and I see her eyes grew dim,
And outside, while I was talkin', sounds the loud Salva-
tion 'ymn.
'Well,' sez she, 'she's gone to glory, and she's up among
the blest,
For it's poor gels like your sister as Lord Jesus likes the
best!'
And from that she got me talkin' ot' *myself,* and when
she 'eard
All my story as I've told yer, up she got without a word,
And she kiss'd me on the forrid! then she sez, 'All that's
gone past!
And there's lots of life before you, now you've come to us
at last!'

Then I larf'd—'I ain't Salvationist, and never mean to
be ;
Tho' a-prayin' and a-singin' may suit *you*, it won't suit
me!'
But she sez, 'You just 'ave patience, for the thing wot's
wrong with *you*
Is just this—you're downright wretched, all for want of
work to do!
One so pretty should be 'appy as a bird upon a tree '
(*Me* pretty! and *me* 'appy!) 'for the Lord, my dear,' sez
she,
' Likes nice cheerful folks about Him, and can't bear to
see them sad,
For He's fond of fun and music, and of everythink that's
glad!"

Well, she got me work, and told me folks must labour
every one,
And 1 said I'd be teetotal (just to please her, and for fun!)
But I allays hated working, and my 'eart felt dull and
low,
And thinks I, 'The publick's better, and religion ain't
no go,'
For somethink black and 'eavy seem'd a-workin' in my
breast,
And I used to go 'ysteric, and I never felt at rest. . . .
But one mornin', when the Army was a-gatherin', I stood
by,
And they 'ollered, 'Glory, glory, to our Father in the
sky!'
And I thought the tune was jolly, and I sang out loud
and gay,
And the minute I begun it, 'arf my trouble pass'd away,
And the louder as I sung it, that great lump I felt inside
Grew a-lighter and a-lighter, while I lep' and sung and
cried!

And when the song was over, up the Captain comes to
　me,
And he sez, 'That voice of yourn, Jane, is as good as any
　three!
Why, you're like a op'ry singer!' he sez, larfin'. . . .
　'Never mind,'
He sez (for I look'd sulky, and his 'art was allays kind!)
'Never mind—there's many among us of such singin'
　would be proud—
He's a long way off, is Jesus, so we've *got* to make it
　loud!"
Then they march'd, and *I* went marchin', for I seem'd
　gone mad that day,
And my 'art inside was dancin' every footstep of the way.
Yes, and that there singin' *saved* me! for the louder as I
　sung,
Why, the more my load was lighten'd, and it seem'd as
　how I sprung
From the ground right up to Jesus, and I 'eard Him
　'oller clear,
'Keep a-marchin' and a-singin', for you've got to get up
　'ere!'"

　　Glory! Hallelujah! March along together!
　　March along, march along, every kind of weather!
　　Wet or dry, shower or shine, ready night and day,
　　Travelling to Jesus, singing on the way!
　　He is waiting for us, yonder in the sky,
　　Stooping down His shining head, to
　　　　　　　　Hear
　　　　　　　　　Our
　　　　　　　　　　Cry!

"Coming back?　Ah, yes, I 'ear them, louder, louder, as
　they come;
Lord, if I might only jine them, march ag'in to fife and
　drum!

. . . I feels faint. . . . A drop o' water!—There, I'm
  better, but my 'ed
Is a-swimmin' to the music. . . . Now it's stop't. . . .
  Wot's that ye said?
They're a-standing 'neath the windy! Lift me up, and let
  me see,
For the sight of them as saved me is like life and breath
  to *me!*
No, I can't!—all's black afore me—and my singin's
  a'most done. . . .
Now, it's lighter! I can see them! all a-standing in the
  sun!
Look, look. it's the Lord Jesus! He's a-formin' them in
  · line,
His white 'orse is golden-bridled, and 'is eyes—see, how
  they shine!
'E's a-speakin'! *Read the Roll-Call!* They're a-throngin'
  one and all,
With their things in marchin' order, they're a-answ'rin' to
  the call.
My turn will soon be comin', for the march must soon
  begin. . . .
'*Alleloojah Jane!* That's *me*, sir! *Ready?* Ready, sir!
  Fall in!"

L'ENVOI TO THE PRECEDING POEM.

NOUGHT is so base that Nature cannot turn
    It's dross to shining gold,
No lamb so lost that it may never learn
    The footpath to the fold.

Be sure this trampled clay beneath our feet
    Hath life as fair as ours,
Be sure this smell of foulness is as sweet
    As scents of fresh young flowers.

All is a mystery and a change,—a strife
    Of evil powers with good :
Sin is the leaven wherewith the bread of life
    Is fashion'd for our food.

God works with instruments as foul as these,
    Sifts Souls from dregs of sense,
Death is his shadow—Sorrow and Disease
    Are both his hand-maidens !

Out of the tangled woof of Day and Night
    His web of Life is spun :
Dust in the beam is just as surely Light
    As yonder shining Sun !

THE GOOD PROFESSOR'S CREED.

(INSCRIBED TO PROFESSOR HUXLEY.)

My creed, without circumlocution,
    I thus deliver clear and pat:
I do believe in Evolution,
    In Protoplasm, and all that!
I do believe in all the 'ologies,
    (Except The-ology, of course!)
But common, cocksure, Useful Knowledge is
    The compass which directs my course.

I don't believe in God or Gammon,
    In powers above or priests below,
But I've some slight respect for Mammon
    As representing *Status quô*;
I hate all efforts revolutionary,
    All systems that subvert the State,
For Law is slow and evolutionary,
    And those low down have got—to wait!

Unless (that fact I should have stated!)
    Unless they're led by Lights like me;
For Evolution, though 'tis fated,
    By gentle Force may further'd be:
In fact, I hold like my existence,
    Since nothing in the world is free,
That Force to which there's no resistance
    Is always justified, *per se*!

I turn from all insipid dishes
    Cook'd by the fools of *Laissez faire*,
And much prefer the loaves and fishes,
    So long as *I* can get my share;

I think the Land is *not* the Nation's,
　But those who grab'd it in the past ;
Statutes, therefore, of limitations,
　Should make all Thieves secure, at last !

I don't believe men free and equal
　(*I* think so ?　Feel my bumps, and tell !)
Of all such fads the sorry sequel
　Is anarchy and social Hell ;
I do believe in " facts " prodigiously,
　Class, label, place them on the shelf,
I do believe (almost religiously !)
　In that most precious Fact, Myself !

I'm many-sided, many-coloured,
　Socialist, Individualist,
I do believe that man a dullard
　Who seeks philanthropies of mist ;
I hold that General Booth's tyrannical,
　And all his scheme of social aid
Is just Religion turn'd mechanical—
　A Barrel-organ badly played !

I think that Liberty's a swindle !
　We look upon it with a smile—
I and my dear Professor Tyndall,
　The Peter Parleys of Carlyle !
He knew the " nigger " was " a servant "
　By law of God, or (what's the same)
By laws proclaimed by prophets fervent
　Of Nature's Tory end and aim !

I turn from every sect and schism,
　God and all gods I leave behind,
I sneer at even Positivism,
　Because it deifies Mankind :

Such creeds are either false or flighty,
  Since men are flesh and flesh is grass,   .
And yet . . . one knowing God Almighty
  Regards me—from the looking-glass!

I do believe that Superstition,
  And what they call " the larger Hope,"
Have fled before the new condition
  Of self-reliance and of soap :
Free from the falsehoods of Divinity,
  Breaking the bonds by preachers spun,
I leave the old creed of the Trinity
  For the new creed of Number One !

Moral and physical diseases
  May be effaced in course of time,
But, left to do whate'er he pleases,
  Man leaps from folly into crime :
We're got to wash and comb and teach him,
  Learn him the laws of self-control,
Wean him from doctrinaires who teach him
  Rubbish about that gas, his Soul !

Be clean, be calm, be thrifty !   These are
  My chief injunctions to the Poor,
Give Cæsar what belongs to Cæsar,
  Don't even begrudge a little more !
Be very careful in your reading,
  Avoid imaginative stuff;
Study the rules of cattle-breeding,
  And when you pair, cry " *quantum suff.*"

To advance the human race I'm willing,
  So long as it is shrewdly done,
But never will I give one shilling
  To any " fad " beneath the sun ;

While the worst fad of all is " Piety,"
   With all its cant of Heaven o'erhead,
Philanthropy's a bad variety
   Of that same fad, when all is said !

And so I sit with calm pulsations,
   Watching the troubled human fry,
Examining their agitations
   With careful microscopic eye !
I, Thomas, *Omnium Scrutator*,
   Finding most creatures mean or base,
Despise your *Hominum Salvator* !
   Man's duty is—to keep his place !

THE BALLAD OF JUDAS ISCARIOT.

'Twas the body of Judas Iscariot
  Lay in the Field of Blood;
'Twas the soul of Judas Iscariot
  Beside the body stood.

Black was the earth by night,
  And black was the sky;
Black, black were the broken clouds,
  Tho' the red Moon went by.

'Twas the body of Judas Iscariot
  Strangled and dead lay there;
'Twas the soul of Judas Iscariot
  Look'd on it in despair.

The breath of the World came and went
  Like a sick man's in rest;
Drop by drop on the World's eyes
  The dews fell cool and blest.

Then the soul of Judas Iscariot
  Did make a gentle moan—
" I will bury underneath the ground
  My flesh and blood and bone.

" I will bury them deep beneath the soil,
  Lest mortals look thereon,
And when the wolf and raven come
  The body will be gone!

" The stones of the field are sharp as steel,
  And hard and cold, God wot;
And I must bear my body hence
  Until I find a spot!"

'Twas the soul of Judas Iscariot,
  So grim, and gaunt, and gray,
Raised the body of Judas Iscariot,
  And carried it away.

And as he bare it from the field
  Its touch was cold as ice,
And the ivory teeth within the jaw
  Rattled aloud, like dice.

As the soul of Judas Iscariot
  Carried its load with pain,
The Eye of Heaven, like a lanthorn's eye,
  Open'd and shut again.

Half he walk'd, and half he seem'd
  Lifted on the cold wind ;
He did not turn, for chilly hands
  Were pushing from behind.

The first place that he came unto
  It was the open wold,
And underneath were prickly whins,
  And a wind that blew so cold.

The next place that he came unto
  It was a stagnant pool,
And when he threw the body in,
  It floated light as wool.

He drew the body on his back,
  And it was dripping chill,
And the next place he came unto
  Was a Cross upon a hill.

A Cross upon the windy hill,
  And a Cross on either side,
Three skeletons that swing thereon,
  Who had been crucified.

And on the middle cross-bar sat
A white Dove slumbering;
Dim it sat in the dim light,
With its head beneath its wing.

And underneath the middle Cross
A grave yawn'd wide and vast,
But the soul of Judas Iscariot
Shiver'd and glided past.

The fourth place that he came unto
It was the Brig of Dread,
And the great torrents rushing down
Were deep, and swift, and red.

He dared not fling the body in
For fear of faces dim,
And arms were waved in the wild water
To thrust it back to him.

'Twas the soul of Judas Iscariot
Turned from the Brig of Dread,
And the dreadful foam of the wild water
Had splash'd the body red.

For days and nights he wander'd on
Upon an open plain,
And the days went by like blinding mist,
And the nights like rushing rain.

For days and nights he wander'd on,
All thro' the Wood of Woe;
And the nights went by like moaning wind,
And the days like drifting snow.

'Twas the soul of Judas Iscariot
Came with a weary face—
Alone, alone, and all alone,
Alone in a lonely place!

He wander'd east, he wander'd west,
 And heard no human sound ;
For months and years, in grief and tears,
 He wander'd round and round.

For months and years, in grief and tears,
 He walk'd the silent night ;
Then the soul of Judas Iscariot
 Perceived a far-off light.

A far-off light across the waste,
 As dim as dim might be,
That came and went like the lighthouse gleam
 On a black night at sea.

'Twas the soul of Judas Iscariot
 Crawl'd to the distant gleam ;
And the rain came down, and the rain was blown
 Against him with a scream.

For days and nights he wander'd on,
 Pushed on by hands behind ;
And the days went by like black, black rain,
 And the nights like rushing wind.

'Twas the soul of Judas Iscariot,
 Strange, and sad, and tall,
Stood all alone at dead of night
 Before a lighted hall.

And the world was white with snow,
 And his foot-marks black and damp,
And the ghost of the silver Moon arose,
 Holding her yellow lamp.

And the icicles were on the eaves,
 And the walls were deep with white,
And the shadows of the guests within
 Pass'd on the window light.

The shadows of the wedding guests
    Did strangely come and go,
And the body of Judas Iscariot
    Lay stretch'd along the snow.

The body of Judas Iscariot
    Lay stretch'd along the snow ;
'Twas the soul of Judas Iscariot
    Ran swiftly to and fro.

To and fro, and up and down,
    He ran so swiftly there,
As round and round the frozen Pole
    Glideth the lean white bear.

'Twas the Bridegroom sat at the table-head,
    And the lights burnt bright and clear—
"Oh, who is that," the Bridegroom said,
    " Whose weary feet I hear ? "

'Twas one who look'd from the lighted hall,
    And answer'd soft and low,
" It is a wolf runs up and down,
    With a black track in the snow."

The Bridegroom in His robe of white
    Sat at the table-head—
"Oh, who is he that moans without ? "
    The blessèd Bridegroom said.

'Twas one who look'd from the lighted hall,
    And answer'd fierce and low,
" 'Tis the soul of Judas Iscariot
    Gliding to and fro."

'Twas the soul of Judas Iscariot
    Did hush itself and stand,
And saw the Bridegroom at the door
    With a light in His hand.

The Bridegroom stood in the open door,
    And He was clad in white,
And far within the Lord's Supper
    Was spread so broad and bright.

The Bridegroom shaded His eyes and look'd,
    And His face was bright to see—
" What dost thou here at the Lord's Supper
    With thy body's sins ? " said He.

'Twas the soul of Judas Iscariot
    Stood black, and sad, and bare—
" I have wander'd many nights and days ;
    There is no light elsewhere."

'Twas the wedding guests cried out within,
    And their eyes were fierce and bright—
" Scourge the soul of Judas Iscariot
    Away into the night ! "

The Bridegroom stood in the open door,
    And He waved hands still and slow,
And the third time that He waved His hands
    The air was thick with snow.

And of every flake of falling snow,
    Before it touch'd the ground,
There came a dove, and a thousand doves
    Made sweet sound.

'Twas the body of Judas Iscariot
    Floated away full fleet,
And the wings of the doves that bare it off
    Were like its winding-sheet.

'Twas the Bridegroom stood at the open door,
    And beckon'd, smiling sweet ;
'Twas the soul of Judas Iscariot
    Stole in, and fell at His feet.

" The Holy Supper is spread within,
   And the many candles shine,
And I have waited long for thee
   Before I pour'd the wine ! "

The supper wine is pour'd at last,
   The lights burn bright and fair,
Iscariot washes the Bridegroom's feet,
   And dries them with his hair.

NIGHTINGALE-SONG.

DEEPER now our raptures grow,
Softlier our voices croon !
Yet more slow
Let our happy music flow,
Sweet and slow, hush'd and low,
Now a dark cloud veils the Moon . . .
Sweet, O sweet !
Watch her while our wild hearts beat ! . . .
See ! she quits the clasping cloud,
Forth she sails on silvern feet,
Smiling, with her bright head bow'd !
Pour the living rapture loud !
Thick and fleet,
Sweet, O sweet !
Now the notes of rapture crowd !

FRA GIACOMO.

I.

ALAS, Fra Giacomo,
  Too late! but follow me . . .
Hush! draw the curtain—so!
  She is dead, quite dead, you see.
Poor little lady! she lies,
All the light gone out of her eyes!
· But her features still wear that soft,
  Gray, meditative expression,
Which you must have noticed oft,
  Thro' the peephole, at confession.
How saintly she looks, how meek!
  Though this be the chamber of death,
  I fancy I feel her breath,
As I kiss her on the cheek.
Too holy for *me*, by far!—
As cold and as pure as a star,
  Not fashioned for kissing and pressing,
But made for a heavenly crown! . . .
Ay, Father, let us go down,—
  But first, if you please, your blessing.

II.

. . . Wine? No! Come, come, you must!
  Blessing it with your prayers,
You'll quaff a cup, I trust,
  To the health of the Saint upstairs.
My heart is aching so!
  And I feel so weary and sad,
  Through the blow that I have had!
You'll sit, Fra Giacomo? . . .

III.

Heigho! 'tis now six summers
 Since I saw that Angel and married her—
 I was passing rich, and I carried her
Off in the face of all comers . . .
So fresh, yet so brimming with Soul !
 A sweeter morsel, I swear,
Never made the dull black coal
 Of a monk's eye glitter and glare . . .
 Your pardon—nay, keep your chair !—
A jest ! but a jest ! . . . Very true,
 It is hardly becoming to jest,
 And that Saint upstairs at rest—
Her Soul may be listening, too !
To think how I doubted and doubted,
Suspected, grumbled at, flouted
That golden-hair'd Angel, and solely
Because she was zealous and holy !—
Night and noon and morn
 She devoted herself to piety—
Not that she seemed to scorn,
 Or shun, her husband's society ;
But the claims of her Soul superseded
All that I asked for or needed,
And her thoughts were far away
From the level of lustful clay,
And she trembled lest earthly matters
Interfered with her *aves* and *paters* !
Sweet dove ! she so fluttered in flying
 To avoid the black vapours of Hell,
So bent on self-sanctifying,
That she never thought of trying
 To save her poor husband as well !
And while she was named and elected
 For place on the heavenly roll,

I (beast that I was) suspected
  Her method of saving her Soul—
So half for the fun of the thing,
What did I (blasphemer) but fling
On my shoulders the gown of a monk,
  (Whom I managed for that very day
  To get safely out of the way),
And seat me, half-sober, half-drunk,
With the cowl drawn over my face,
In the Father Confessor's place . . .
Eheu! benedicite!
In her beautiful sweet simplicity,
With that pensive gray expression,
She sighfully knelt at confession,—
While I bit my lips till they bled,
  And dug my nails in my palm,
And heard, with averted head,
  The horrible words come calm—
Each word was a serpent's sting ;
  But, wrapt in my gloomy gown,
I sat like a marble thing
  As she uttered *your* name. Sɪᴛ ᴅᴏᴡɴ !

IV.

More wine, Fra Giacomo ?
One cup—as you love me ! No ?
Come, drink ! 'twill bring the streaks
Of crimson back to your cheeks.
Come ! drink again to the Saint,
Whose virtues you loved to paint,
Who, stretched on her wifely bed,
  With the soft, sweet, gray expression
  You saw and admired at confession—
Lies *poisoned*, overhead !

V.

Sit still—or, by God, you die!
Face to face, soul to soul, you and I
    Have settled accounts, in a fine
    Pleasant fashion, over our wine—
Stir not, and seek not to fly—
    Nay, whether or not, you are mine!
Thank Montepulciano for giving
    Your death in such delicate sips—
'Tis not every monk ceases living
    With so pleasant a taste on his lips—
But lest Montepulciano unsurely should kiss,
    Take this!—and this!—and this!

VI.

. . . Raise him; and cast him, Pietro,
Into the deep canal below:
You can be secret, lad, I know . . .
And, hark you, then to the convent go—
Bid every bell of the convent toll,
And the monks say mass, for your Mistress's soul.

CHARMIAN.

Cleo. Charmian !
Char. Madam?
Cleo. Give me to drink mandragora !
Anthony and Cleopatra.

In the time when water-lilies shake
Their green and gold on river and lake,
When the cuckoo calls in the heart o' the heat,
When the Dog-star foams and the shade is sweet ;
Where cool and fresh the River ran,
I sat by the side of the Charmian,
And heard no sound from the world of Man.

All was so sweet and still that day !
The rustling shade, the rippling stream,
All life, all breath dissolved away
Into a golden dream ;
Warm and sweet the scented shade
Drowsily caught the breeze and stirred,
Faint and low through the green glade
Came hum of bee and song of bird.
Our hearts were full of sleepy bliss,
And yet we did not clasp or kiss,
Nor did we break the happy spell
With tender tone or syllable.
But to ease our hearts and set thought free,
We pluckt the flowers of a red rose-tree,
And, leaf by leaf, we threw them, Sweet,
Into the River at our feet,
And in an indolent delight
Watch'd them glide onward, slowly, out of sight.

Sweet, had I spoken boldly then,
How might my love have garner'd thee !
But I had left the paths of men,
And sitting yonder, dreamily,
Was happiness enough for me !
Seeking no gift of word or kiss,
But looking in thy face, was bliss !
Plucking the rose-leaves in a dream,
Watching them glimmer down the stream,
Knowing that eastern heart of thine
Shared the dim ecstasy of mine !

Then, while we linger'd, cold and gray
Came Twilight, chilling soul and sense ;
And you arose to go away,
Full of divine indifference !
I missed the spell—I watched it break,—
And such come never twice to man :
In a less golden hour I spake,
And did *not* win thee, Charmian !

For wearily we turned away
Into the world of everyday,
And from thy heart the fancy fled
Like the rose-leaves on the River shed ;
But to me that hour is sweeter far
Than the world and all its treasures are :
Still to sit on, so close to thee,
Were Paradise enough for me !
Still to sit on, in a green nook,
Nor break the spell by word or look !
To reach out happy hands for ever,
To pluck the rose-leaves, Charmian !
To watch them fade on the gleaming River,
And hear no sound from the world of Man !

THE WAKE OF O'HARA.

(SEVEN DIALS).

To the Wake of O'Hara
    Came companie;
All St. Patrick's Alley
    Was there to see,
With the friends and kinsmen
    Of the family.
On the long deal table lay Tim in white,
And at his pillow the burning light.
Pale as himself, with the tears on her cheek,
The mother received us, too full to speak;
But she heap'd the fire, and on the board
Set the black bottle with never a word,
While the company gather'd, one and all,
Men and women, big and small—
Not one in the Alley but felt a call
    To the Wake of Tim O'Hara.

At the face of O'Hara,
    All white with sleep,
Not one of the women
    But took a peep,
And the wives new-wedded
    Began to weep.
The mothers gather'd round about,
And praised the linen and laying-out,—
For white as snow was his winding-sheet,
And all was peaceful, and clean, and sweet;
And the old wives, praising the blessèd dead,
Were thronging round the old press-bed,

Where O'Hara's widow, tatter'd and torn,
Held to her bosom the babe new-born,
And stared all around her, with eyes forlorn,
 At the Wake of Tim O'Hara.

  For the heart of O'Hara
   Was good as gold,
  And the life of O'Hara
   Was bright and bold,—
  The boy was the darling
   Of young and old !
Gay as a guinea, wet or dry,
With a smiling mouth and a twinkling eye !
Had ever an answer for chaff and fun ;
Would fight like a lion, with any one !
Not a neighbour of any trade
But knew some joke that the boy had made;
Not a neighbour, dull or bright,
But minded *something*—frolic or fight,
And whisper'd it round the fire that night,
 At the Wake of Tim O'Hara !

  " To God be glory
   In death and life,
  He's taken O'Hara
   From throuble and strife ! "
  Said one-eyed Biddy,
   The apple-wife.
" God bless ould Ireland ! " said Mistress Hart,
Mother to Mike of the donkey-cart ;
" God bless ould Ireland till all be done,
She never made wake for a better son ! "
And all join'd chorus, and each one said
Something kind of the boy that was dead;
And the bottle went round from lip to lip,
And the weeping widow, for fellowship,

Took the glass of old Biddy and had a sip,
  At the Wake of Tim O'Hara.

      Then we drank to O'Hara,
        With drams to the brim,
      While the face of O'Hara
        Look'd on so grim,
      In the corpse-light shining
        Yellow and dim.
The cup of liquor went round again,
And the talk grew louder at every drain ;
Louder the tongues of the women grew !—
The lips of the boys were loosening too !
The widow her weary eyelids closed,
And, soothed by the drop o' drink, she dozed :
The mother brighten'd and laugh'd to hear
Of O'Hara's fight with the grenadier,
And the hearts of all took better cheer,
      At the Wake of Tim O'Hara.

      Tho' the face of O'Hara
        Lookt on so wan,
      In the chimney-corner
        The row began—
      Lame Tony was in it,
        The oyster-man ;
For a dirty low thief from the North came near,
And whistled "Boyne Water" in his ear,
And Tony, with never a word of grace,
Flung out his fist in the blackguard's face ;
And the girls and women scream'd out for fright,
And the men that were drunkest began to fight,—
Over the tables and chairs they threw,—
The corpse-light tumbled,—the shindy grew,—
The new-born join'd in the hullabaloo,—
      At the Wake of Tim O'Hara.

"Be still! be silent!
    Ye do a sin!
Shame be his portion
    Who dares begin!"
'Twas Father O'Connor
    Just enter'd in!—
All look'd down, and the row was done—
And shamed and sorry was every one;
But the Priest just smiled quite easy and free—
"Would ye wake the poor boy from his sleep?" said he :
And he said a prayer, with a shining face,
Till a kind of a brightness fill'd the place;
The women lit up the dim corpse-light,
The men were quieter at the sight,
And the peace of the Lord fell on all that night
        At the Wake of Tim O'Hara!

THE WEDDING OF SHON MACLEAN.

A BAGPIPE BALLAD.

To the Wedding of Shon Maclean,
　　Twenty Pipers together
Came in the wind and the rain
　　Playing across the heather;
Backward their ribbons flew,
Blast upon blast they blew,
Each clad in tartan new,
　　Bonnet, and blackcock feather:
And every Piper was fou,*
　　Twenty Pipers together! . . .

He's but a Sassenach blind and vain
Who never heard of Shon Maclean—
The Duke's own Piper, called "Shon the Fair,"
From his freckled skin and his fiery hair.
Father and son, since the world's creation,
The Macleans had followed this occupation,
And played the pibroch to fire the clan
Since the first Duke came and the Earth began.
Like the whistling of birds, like the humming of
　　bees,
Like the sough of the south-wind in the trees,
Like the singing of angels, the playing of shawms,
Like Ocean itself with its storms and its calms,
Were the strains of Shon, when with cheeks
　　aflame
He blew a blast thro' the pipes of fame.

---

* Pronounce *foo*—*i.e.*, 'half seas over,' intoxicated.

At last, in the prime of his playing life,
The spirit moved him to take a wife—
A lassie with eyes of Highland blue,
Who love the pipes and the Piper too,
And danced to the sound, with a foot and a leg
White as a lily and smooth as an egg.
So, twenty Pipers were coming together
O'er the moor and across the heather,
    All in the wind and the rain :
Twenty Pipers so brawly dressed
Were flocking in from the east and the west,
To bless the bedding and blow their best
    At the Wedding of Shon Maclean.

At the Wedding of Shon Maclean
    'Twas wet and windy weather !
Yet, thro' the wind and the rain
    Came twenty Pipers together !
Earach and Dougal Dhu,
Sandy of Isla too,
Each with the bonnet o' blue,
    Tartan, and blackcock feather :
And every Piper was fou,
    Twenty Pipers together !

The knot was tied, the blessing said,
Shon was married, the feast was spread.
At the head of the table sat, huge and hoar,
Strong Sandy of Isla, age fourscore,
Whisker'd, grey as a Haskeir seal,
And clad in crimson from head to heel
Beneath and round him in their degree
Gathered the men of minstrelsie,
With keepers, gillies, and lads and lasses,
Mingling voices, and jingling glasses.

At soup and haggis, at roast and boil'd,
Awhile the happy gathering toil'd,—
While Shon and Jean at the table ends
Shook hands with a hundred of their friends.—
Then came a hush. Thro' the open door
A wee bright form flash'd on the floor,—
The Duke himself, in the kilt and plaid,
With slim soft knees, like the knees of a maid.
And he took a glass, and he cried out plain,
" I drink to the health of Shon Maclean !
To Shon the Piper and Jean his wife,
A clean fireside and a merry life ! "
Then out he slipt, and each man sprang
To his feet, and with " hooch " the chamber rang !
" Clear the tables ! " shriek'd out one—
A leap, a scramble,—and it was done !
And then the Pipers all in a row
Tuned their pipes and began to blow,
    While all to dance stood fain :
Sandy of Isla and Earach More,
Dougal Dhu from Kilflannan shore,
Played up the company on the floor
    At the Wedding of Shon Maclean.

At the Wedding of Shon Maclean,
    Twenty Pipers together
Stood up, while all their train
    Ceased to clatter and blether.
Full of the mountain-dew,
First in their pipes they blew,
Mighty of bone and thew,
    Red-cheek'd, with lungs of leather :
And every Piper was fou,
    Twenty Pipers together !

Who led the dance ? In pomp and pride
The Duke himself led out the Bride !
Great was the joy of each beholder,
For the wee Duke only reach'd her shoulder ;
And they danced, and turned, when the reel began,
Like a giantess and a fairie man !
But like an earthquake was the din
When Shon himself led the Duchess in !
And she took her place before him there,
Like a white mouse dancing with a bear !
So trim and tiny, so slim and sweet,
Her blue eyes watching Shon's great feet,
With a smile that could not be resisted,
She jigged, and jumped, and twirl'd, and twisted !
Sandy of Isla led off the reel,
The Duke began it with toe and heel,
  Then all join'd in amain ;
Twenty Pipers ranged in a row,
From squinting Shamus to lame Kilcroe,
Their cheeks like crimson, began to blow,
  At the Wedding of Shon Maclean.

  At the Wedding of Shon Maclean
   They blew with their lungs of leather,
  And blithesome was the strain
   Those Pipers played together !
  Moist with the mountain dew,
  Mighty of bone and thew,
  Each with the bonnet o' blue,
   Tartan, and blackcock feather :
  And every Piper was fou,
   Twenty Pipers together !

Oh for a wizard's tongue to tell
Of all the wonders that befel !

Of how the Duke, when the first stave died,
Reached up on tiptoe to kiss the Bride,
While Sandy's pipes, as their mouths were meeting,
Skirl'd, and set every heart abeating!
Then Shon took the pipes! and all was still,
As silently he the bags did fill,
With flaming cheeks and round bright eyes,
Till the first faint music began to rise.
Like a thousand laverocks singing in tune,
Like countless corn-craiks under the moon,
Like the smack of kisses, like kirk bells ringing,
Like a mermaid's harp, or a kelpie singing,
Blew the pipes of Shon ; and the witching strain
Was the gathering song of the Clan Maclean!
Then slowly, softly, at his side,
All the Pipers around replied,
     And swelled the solemn strain :
The hearts of all were proud and light,
To hear the music, to see the sight,
And the Duke's own eyes were dim that night,
     At the Wedding of Shon Maclean.

     So to honour the Clan Maclean
          Straight they began to gather,
     Blowing the wild refrain,
     " Blue bonnets across the heather ! "
     They stamp'd, they strutted, they blew ;
     They shriek'd ; like cocks they crew ;
     Blowing the notes out true,
          With wonderful lungs of leather :
     And every Piper was fou,
          Twenty Pipers together !

When the Duke and Duchess went away
The dance grew mad and the guests grew gay ;

Man and maiden, face to face,
Leapt and footed and scream'd apace!
Round and round the dancers whirl'd,
Shriller, louder, the Pipers skirl'd,
Till the soul seem'd swooning into sound,
And all Creation was whirling round!
Then, in a pause of the dance and glee,
The Pipers, ceasing their minstrelsie,
Draining the glass in groups did stand,
And passed the sneesh-box* from hand to hand.
Sandy of Isla, with locks of snow,
Squinting Shamus, blind Kilmahoe,
Finlay Beg, and Earach More,
Dougal Dhu of Kilflannan shore—
All the Pipers, black, yellow, and green,
All the colours that ever were seen,
All the Pipers of all the Macs,
Gather'd together and took their cracks. †
Then (no man knows how the thing befel,
For none was sober enough to tell)
These heavenly Pipers from twenty places
Began disputing with crimson faces;
Each asserting, like one demented,
The claims of the Clan *he* represented.
In vain grey Sandy of Isla strove
To soothe their struggle with words of love,
Asserting there, like a gentleman,
The superior claims of his own great Clan;
Then, finding to reason is despair,
He seizes his pipes and plays an air—
The gathering tune of his Clan—and tries
To drown in music the shrieks and cries!
Heavens! Every Piper, grown mad with ire,
Seizes *his* pipes with a fierce desire,

Snuff-box.   † Conversed sociably.

And blowing madly, with skirl and squeak,
Begins *his* particular tune to shriek !
Up and down the gamut they go,
Twenty Pipers, all in a row,
   Each with a different strain !
Each tries hard to drown the first,
Each blows louder till like to burst.
Thus were the tunes of the Clans rehearst
   At the Wedding of Shon Maclean !

At the Wedding of Shon Maclean,
   Twenty Pipers together,
Blowing with might and main,
   Thro' wonderful lungs of leather !
Wild was the hullabaloo !
They stamp'd, they scream'd, they crew !
Twenty strong blasts they blew,
   Holding the heart in tether :
And every Piper was fou,
   Twenty Pipers together !

A storm of music ! Like wild sleuth-hounds
Contending together, were the sounds !
At last a bevy of Eve's bright daughters
Pour'd oil—that's whisky—upon the waters ;
And after another dram went down
The Pipers chuckled and ceased to frown,
Embraced like brothers and kindred spirits,
And fully admitted each other's merits.
All bliss must end ! For now the Bride
Was looking weary and heavy-eyed,
And soon she stole from the drinking chorus,
While the company settled to *deoch-an-dorus.**

---

* The parting glass ; lit. the *cup at the door.*

One hour—another—took its flight—
The clock struck twelve—the dead of night—
And still the Bride like a rose so red
Lay lonely up in the bridal bed.
At half-past two the Bridegroom, Shon,
Dropt on the table as heavy as stone,
But four strong Pipers across the floor
Carried him up to the bridal door,
Push'd him in at the open portal,
And left him snoring, serene and mortal!
The small stars twinkled over the heather,
As the Pipers wandered away together,
But one by one on the journey dropt,
Clutching his pipes, and there he stopt!
One by one on the dark hillside
Each faint blast of the bagpipes died,
    Amid the wind and the rain!
And the twenty Pipers at break of day
In twenty different bogholes lay,
Serenely sleeping upon their way
    From the Wedding of Shon Maclean!

PHIL BLOOD'S LEAP.

THERE's some think Injins pison, and others count 'em
    scum,
And night and day they are melting away, clean into
    Kingdom Come ;
But don't you go and make mistakes, like many dern'd
    fools I've known,
For dirt is dirt, and snakes is snakes, but an Injin's flesh
    and bone !

We were seeking gold in the Texan hold, and we'd had a
    blaze of luck,
More rich and rare the stuff ran there at every foot we
    struck ;
Like men gone wild we t'iled and t'iled, and never
    seemed to tire,
The hot sun beamed, and our faces streamed with the
    sweat of a mad desire.

I was Captain then of the mining men, and I had a
    precious life,
For a wilder set I never met at derringer and knife ;
Nigh every day there was some new fray, a bullet in
    some one's brain,
And the viciousest brute to stab and to shoot was an
    Imp of Hell from Maine.

Phil Blood. Well, he was six foot three, with a squint
    to make you skeer'd,
His face all scabb'd, and twisted and stabb'd, with carroty
    hair and beard,
Sour as the drink in Bitter Chink, sharp as a grizzly's
    squeal,
Limp in one leg, for a leaden egg had nick'd him in the
    heel.

No beauty was he, but a sight to see, all stript to the
waist and bare,
With his grim-set jaws, and his panther claws, and his
hawk's eye all aglare;
With pick and spade in sun and shade he laboured like
darnation,
But when his spell was over,--well! he was fond of his
recreation!

And being a crusty kind of cuss, the only sport he had,
When work was over, seemed to *us* a bit too rough and
bad;
For to put some lead in a comrade's head was the greatest
fun in life,
And the sharpest joke he was known to poke was the
p'int of his precious knife.

But game to the bone was Phil, I'll own, and he always
fought most fair,
With as good a will to be killed as kill, true grit as any
there:
Of honour too, like me or you, he'd a scent, though not
so keen,
Would rather be riddled thro' and thro' than do what he
thought mean.

But his eddication to his ruination had not been over
nice,
And his stupid skull was choking full of vulgar pre-
judice;
With anything white he'd drink, or he'd fight in fair and
open fray;
But to murder and kill was his wicked will, if an Injin
came his way!

" A sarpent's hide has pison inside, and an Injin's heart's
    the same,
If he seems your friend for to gain his end, look out for
    the sarpent's game ;
Of the snakes that crawl, the worst of all is the snake in
    a skin of red,
A spotted Snake, and no mistake?" that's what he always
    said.

Well, we'd jest struck our bit of luck, and were wild as
    raving men,
When, who should stray to our camp one day, but Black
    Panther, the Cheyenne ;
Drest like a Christian, all a-grin, the old one joins our
    band,
And tho' the rest look'd black as sin, he shakes *me* by the
    hand.

Now, the poor old cuss had been good to us, and I knew
    that he was true,—
I'd have trusted him with life and limb as soon as I'd
    trust *you ;*
For tho' his wit was gone a bit, and he drank like any
    fish,
His heart was kind, he was well-inclined, as even a white
    could wish.

Food had got low, for we didn't know the run of the
    hunting ground,
And our hunters were sick, when, jest in the nick, the
    friend in need was found ;
For he knew the place like his mother's face (or better, a
    heap, you'd say,
Since she was a squaw of the roaming race, and himself
    a cast-away).

Well, I took the Panther into camp, and the critter was
　　well content,
And off with him, on the hunting tramp, next day our
　　hunters went,
And I reckon that day and the next we didn't want for
　　food,
And only one in the camp looked vext—that Imp of Hell,
　　Phil Blood.

Nothing would please his contrairy idees! an Injin made
　　him rile !
He didn't speak, but I saw on his cheek a kind of an
　　ugly smile ;
And I knew his skin was hatching sin, and I kept the
　　Panther apart,
For the Injin he was too blind to see the dirt in a white
　　man's heart !

Well, one fine day, we a-resting lay at noon-time by the
　　creek,
The red sun blazed, and we felt half-dazed, too beat to
　　stir or speak ;
'Neath the alder trees we stretched at ease, and we
　　couldn't see the sky,
For the lian-flowers in bright blue showers hung through
　　the boughs on high.

It was like the gleam of a fairy dream, and I felt like
　　earth's first Man,
In an Eden bower, with the yellow flower of a cactus for
　　a fan ;
Oranges, peaches, grapes, and figs, cluster'd, ripen'd, and
　　fell,
And the cedar scent was pleasant, blent with the soothing
　　'cacia smell.

The squirrels red ran overhead, and I saw the lizards
  creep,
And the woodpecker bright with the chest so white tapt
  like a sound in sleep;
I dreamed and dozed with eyes half-closed, and felt like
  a three-year child,
And, a plantain blade on his brow for a shade, even Phil
  Blood look'd mild.

Well, back, jest then, came our hunting men, with the
  Panther at their head,
Full of his fun was every one, and the Panther's eyes
  were red,
And he skipt about with grin and shout, for he'd had a
  drop that day,
And he twisted and twirled, and squeal'd and skirl'd, in
  the foolish Injin way.

To the waist all bare Phil Blood lay there, with only his
  knife in his belt,
And I saw his bloodshot eye-balls stare, and I knew how
  ugly he felt,—
When the Injin dances with grinning glances around him
  as he lies,
With his painted skin and his monkey grin,—and leers
  into his eyes!

Then before I knew what I should do Phil Blood was on
  his feet,
And the Injin could trace the hate in his face, and his
  heart began to beat,
And, "Git out o' the way," he heard them say, "for he
  means to hev your life!"
But before he could fly at the warning cry, he saw the
  flash of the knife.

"Run, Panther, run!" cried each mother's son, and the
    Panther took the track ;
With a wicked glare, like a wounded bear, Phil Blood
    sprang at his back.
Up the side so steep of the cañon deep the poor old
    critter sped,
And the devil's limb ran after him, till they faded over-
    head.

Now, the spot of ground where our luck was found was a
    queerish place, you'll mark,
Jest under the jags of the mountain crags and the preci-
    pices dark,
Far up on high, close to the sky, the two crags leant to-
    gether,
Leaving a gap, like an open trap, with a gleam of golden
    weather.

A pathway led from the beck's dark bed up to the crags
    on high,
And along that path the Injin fled, fast as a man could
    fly.
Some shots were fired, for I desired to keep the white
    beast back ;
But I missed my man, and away he ran on the flying
    Injin's track.

Now all below is thick, you know, with 'cacia, alder, and
    pine,
And the bright shrubs deck the side of the beck, and the
    lian flowers so fine,
For the forest creeps all under the steeps, and feathers
    the feet of the crags
With boughs so thick that your path you pick like a
    steamer among the snags.

But right above you, the crags, Lord love you! are bare
    as this here hand,
And your eyes you wink at the bright blue chink, as
    looking up you stand.
If a man should pop in that trap at the top, he'd never
    rest arm or leg,
Till neck and crop to the bottom he'd drop—and smash
    on the stones like an egg!

" Come back, you cuss! come back to us! and let the
    critter be!"
I screamed out loud, while the men in a crowd stood
    grinning at them and me . . .
But up they went, and my shots were spent, and at last
    they disappeared,—
One minute more, and we gave a roar, for the Injin had
    leapt,—and *cleared*!

A leap for a deer, not a man, to clear,—and the bloodiest
    grave below!
But the critter was smart and mad with fear, and he went
    like a bolt from a bow!
Close after him came the devil's limb, with his face set
    grim as death,
But when he came to the gulch's brim, I reckon he paused
    for breath!

For breath at the brink! but—a white man shrink, when
    a red had passed so neat?
I knew Phil Blood too well to think he'd turn his back
    dead beat!
He takes one run, leaps up in the sun, and bounds from
    the slippery ledge,
And he clears the hole, but—God help his soul!—just
    touches the tother edge!

One scrambling fall, one shriek, one call, from the men
　　that stand and stare,—
Black in the blue where the sky looks thro', he staggers,
　　dwarf'd up there;
The edge he touches, then sinks, and clutches the rock
　　—our eyes grow dim—
I turn away—what's that they say?—he's a-hanging on
　　to the brim!

. . . On the very brink of the fatal chink a ragged
　　shrub there grew,
And to that he clung, and in silence swung betwixt us
　　and the blue,
And as soon as a man could run I ran the way I'd seen
　　them flee,
And I came mad-eyed to the chasm's side, and—what do
　　you think I see?

All up? Not quite. Still hanging? Right! But he'd torn
　　away the shrub;
With lolling tongue he clutch'd and swung—to what?
　　ay, that's the rub!
I saw him glare and dangle in air,—for the empty hole he
　　trode,—
Help'd by a *pair of hands* up there!—The Injin's? Yes,
　　by God!

Now boys, look here! for many a year I've roam'd in
　　this here land—
And many a sight both day and night I've seen that I
　　think grand;
Over the whole wide world I've been, and I know both
　　things and men,
But the biggest sight I've ever seen was the sight I saw
　　jest then.

I held my breath—so nigh to death Phil Blood swung
  hand and limb,
And it seemed to us all that down he'd fall, with the
  Panther after him,
But the Injin at length put out his strength—and another
  moment past,—
—Then safe and sound to the solid ground he drew Phil
  Blood, at last!!

Saved? True for you! By an Injin too!—and the man
  he meant to kill!
There, all alone, on the brink of stone, I see them standing still;
Phil Blood gone white, with the struggle and fright, like
  a great mad bull at bay,
And the Injin meanwhile, with a half-skeer'd smile, ready
  to spring away.

What did Phil do? Well, I watched the two, and I saw
  Phil Blood turn back,
Bend over the brink and take a blink right down the
  chasm black,
Then stooping low for a moment or so, he sheath'd his
  bowie bright,
Spat slowly down, and watch'd with a frown, as the
  spittle sank from sight!

Hands in his pockets, eyes downcast, silent, thoughtful,
  and grim,
While the Panther, grinning as he passed, still kept his
  eyes on him,
Phil Blood strolled slow to his mates below, down by the
  mountain track,
With his lips set tight and his face all white, and the
  Panther at his back.

I reckon they stared when the two appeared! but never
   a word Phil spoke,
Some of them laughed and others jeered,—but he let
   them have their joke;
He seemed amazed, like a man gone dazed, the sun in his
   eyes too bright,
And for many a week, in spite of their cheek, he never
   offered to fight.

And after that day he changed his play, and kept a
   civiller tongue,
And whenever an Injin came that way, his contrairy head
   he hung;
But whenever he heard the lying word, "*It's a* Lie!"
   Phil Blood would groan;
"*A Snake is a Snake, make no mistake! but an Injin's
flesh and bone!*"

THE GOLDEN YEAR:

Now the winter of sorrow is over,
    And the season of waiting is done,
'Mid acclaim of the people who love her
    Our Lady steps forth in the sun ;
The green earth beneath and the blue sky above her,
She walks in the sight of the millions who cover
    The realms she hath welded to one !
'Tis Jubilee here, and 'tis Jubilee yonder,
As far as the sun round her empire doth wander,
From the east to the west wakes the world in her honour,
The sunrise and sunset flash splendour upon her,
    Now winter is over and done !

. . . Empress and Queen, the flowers and fruits of nations
    Are heapt upon the footstool of thy throne ;
Amid the thronging hosts, the acclamations,
    The trumpets of thy Jubilee are blown !
Glorious and glad, with pomp and pride resplendent,
Thy subject Spirits come and wait attendant :
Tawny and proud, a queenly sibyl-maiden,
    ' Comes INDIA, clad in woofs of strange device,
With fruitage from the fabled Eastern Aiden,
    And gifts of precious gems and gold and spice ;
On a white elephant she rides, while round her
    Like baying hounds her spotted tigers run—
Black-brow'd as night, to her who tamed and crown'd her
    She comes, with fiery eyes that front the sun.
AUSTRALIA follows, in a chariot golden
    Drawn by black heifers ; on the chariot's side
An ocean eagle sits with white wings folden,
    And o'er her head float egrets purple-dyed.

E

Tatoo'd Tasmania, with wild ringlets flowing,
  Followed by savage herds and hinds, strides near.
Canada's comes mocassin'd, clearly blowing
  Her forest horn, and brandishing her spear.
Albion in martial mail, with trident gleaming,
  Leads an old lion, and a lamb snow-white;
Blonde Caledonia, with glad tartan streaming
  Back from her shoulder, leaves her lonely height,
And with her mountain Sister, to the strumming
  Of harp and pipe, joins the rejoicing throng.
The world is shadow'd with the swarms still coming
  To hail their Queen with mirth and festal song!

  For the winter of sorrow is over,
   And gone are the griefs that have been,
  'Mid acclaim of the people who love her
   She comes to her glory, a Queen.
'Tis Jubilee here, and 'tis Jubilee yonder
As far as the sun round her empire doth wander,
From the east to the west wakes the world in her
 honour,
The sunrise and sunset flash splendour upon her,
  Unclouded, at peace, and serene!

Yet . . . who is this that rises up before her,
  Ragged and hungry, blood upon her hands?
Smileless beneath the heavens now smiling o'er her,
  Wild grey-hair'd Erin on her island stands!
Loudly she crieth, " Crownèd Queen and Mother,
  If such thou art, redress my children's wrong;
Upraise the seed of Esau! Bid his brother
  Restore to him the birthright stol'n so long!
'Mid his fat flocks sits Jacob unrepenting,
  Yet starts with lifted wine-cup at my cry;
My children starve—my tribe is left lamenting—
  My dwellings lie unroof'd beneath the sky.

Even the mess of pottage gives he never,
 For which he bought the birthright long ago ;
While joy in Jacob's vineyard flows for ever,
 Esau preserves his heritage of woe !
Justice, O Queen, or ——" For the rest she clutches
 Her naked knife, and laughs in shrill despair. . . .
O Queen and Empress, by the piteous touches
 Of Love's anointing fingers, hear her prayer !
Let not thy Jubilee be stained, O Mother,
 By the old sin the sinful past hath known.
The wrongs this Esau suffers from his brother
 Are blood-stains on the brightness of thy throne !

  Now the winter of sorrow is ended,
   And the season of waiting is fled;
  Let the blessing by all men attended
   On Esau and Erin be shed !
'Tis Jubilee here, and 'tis Jubilee yonder
As far as the sun round thine empire doth wander ;
But Esau roams outcast and homeless, O Mother,—
At night on the rocks, near the tents of his brother,
   The weary one pillows his head !

O bright and beauteous, Lady, is thy splendour,
 The waves of life leap round thee like a sea—
Smiling thou hearest, happy-eyed and tender,
 The silver clarions of thy Jubilee !
And yet . . . O God ! what shrouded shapes of pity
 Are these who cry unto thee from afar ?
Huddling beneath the gas, in the dark City,
 Hagar and Mary wail their evil star !
For Hagar still is hungry and forth-driven,
 And Magdalen still crawls from door to door,
Tho' He who cast no stone, and promised Heaven,
 Bade her repent and go, and sin no more.

Long, long hath she repented, tho' foul fetters
    Still bind her to the sin without a name ;
And on the children's breasts the crimson letters
    Tell to a cruel world the mother's shame.
But *thou*, too, art a Mother, Queen appointed,
    And *thou*, too, hast thy children ! Wherefore, heed
The crying of the lost one, who anointed
    Thy Master's feet, and save her sinless seed.
Feed Hagar and her little ones, whose crying
    Pierces the heart of Pity to the core !
Find Magdalen, from shrine to shrine still flying,
    And say to him who stones her as of yore :
" The time hath come for justice in full measure,
    For him who shares the sin to share the stain ;
No longer shall my triumph or my pleasure
    Be troubled by my broken sister's pain ! "
O Lady, such a word of vindication
    Shall value all thy splendour twentyfold ;
Hagar's new gladness, Magdalen's salvation,
    Would be a brighter crown than that of gold !

    . . .   For the season of waiting is over,
            And the winter of sorrow is done,
        'Mid acclaim of the people who love her
            Our Lady steps forth in the sun.
    'Tis Jubilee here, and 'tis Jubilee yonder
    As far as the sun round her empire doth wander,
    If the weary and outcast are weeping no longer,
    The wrong'd stands erect, at her feet kneels the
            wronger,
        For the Golden Year has begun !

The Golden Year ! How loudly and how gladly
    The trumpets of thy Jubilee are blown !
But . . . what is this that loometh out so sadly
    Yonder, behind the shining of thy throne ?

Christ's Tree? A cloud of blackness doth enfold it,
  Beneath it weeping shapes their wild arms toss—
Alas! the bright sun strikes, and we behold it—
  The Tree of Man's Invention, not the Cross!
Blackest of blots upon thy throne pure golden
  Casts this foul growth of evil, with its root
Deep as the roots of Hell, this upas olden
  With blood for blossoms, flesh and blood for fruit!
And weeping angels of the empyræan
  Look down in shame and sorrow from the sky,
While followers of the bloodless Galilean
  With impious rites lead deathless Cain to die!
While this Tree bears, O Queen, while earth is sooted
  With its black shadow, woe to thine and thee!
The air around thy throne shall be polluted,
  And Hell must laugh to hear thy Jubilee!

    By the hope and the faith thou dost cherish,
      By summer now breaking serene,
    Let the Tree of man's cruelty perish,
      The Cross of man's mercy be seen!
  'Tis Jubilee here, and 'tis Jubilee yonder,
  As far as the sun round thine empire doth wander,
  But, long as these boughs of the upas are bearing,
  The sound of sad weeping, of bitter despairing,
      Shall trouble thy glory, O Queen!

O merry music! Drums and fifes are sounding,
  Thy realm is resonant from sea to sea!
A million hearts are gladdening and bounding
  To the great glory of thy Jubilee!
Yet . . . who are these that thy proud throne environ,
  That, ring'd around by swords, with shout and laugh
Drag forth the monsters from whose mouths of iron
  The frail Sepoy was blown like bloodiest chaff?

Thy warriors? Thine? Not His who came proclaiming
   Love's gospel, while earth's Kings knelt down to
     hear?
O Queen, then Fire and Sword surround thee, shaming
   The peace and plenty of thy Golden Year?
O hearken! From the lonely desert places,
   From graves thy hosts have dug these latter years,
The cry of wailing tribes and wounded races
   Breaks on thy queendom with a sound of tears;
And while in cottages and princely towers
   Pale English widows weep and orphans moan,
Death comes to set his pallid funeral flowers
   And yew-trees round the footstool of thy throne!

     Yet gone are the seasons of sorrow
       And winter hath vanish'd (men say)!
     Shall Famine and Fire come to-morrow
       And add to the graves of to-day?
'Tis Jubilee here, and 'tis Jubilee yonder,
As far as the sun round thine empire doth wander,
Yet Cain rears his altar and slays his frail brother,
And men who should cherish and love one another
     Go smiling to torture and slay!

Listen, O Empress, to the tearful voices
   That pierce above the thunder of thy State!
Beyond the throng that gladdens and rejoices
   The flocks of human martyrs weep and wait.
They know thee great and good, O Queen and Mother,
   They hunger for the blessing of thy hand;
But Jacob in his pride forgets his brother,
   And Hagar wanders famish'd thro' the land.
Grasping thine Aaron's rod with gentle fingers,
   Touch hearts of stone until the fountains start,
Shed summer on the isle where winter lingers,
   Fill the black void in Erin's aching heart!

Rebuke thy legions! Bid them crouch before thee,
    Nor lusting still for conquest draw the sword!
Let doves, not battle-ravens, hover o'er thee,
    And Christ, not Moloch, deck thy festal board!
For all this pomp and pride turn black and bitter
    If women weep and mourners wail their dead,
The blessing of the sorrowful were fitter
    To crown thee than the crown upon thy head!
O hearken yet, this year of years, O Mother,
    Proclaim sweet peace from every heaven-lit hill,
Let Justice be thy handmaid, and no other,
    And say to all things evil, " Cease, be still ! "

      O then shall all sorrow be over,
        And then indeed winter be done,
      'Mid acclaim of the people who love her
        Our Lady shall walk in the sun!
The green earth beneath and the blue sky above
    her,
Her smile shall shed peace on the millions who cover
      The realms she hath welded to one.
'Tis Jubilee here, and 'tis Jubilee yonder
As far as the sun round her empire doth wander,
But Jubilee brighter shall come with to-morrow,
With the end of all strife and surcease of all sorrow,
      When the night-tide of evil is done!

            Epode.

LADY, God lends a torch to light
    Thy path to peace transcending dreams.
Uphold it! See, from height to height,
Across the day, across the night,
    Its splendour streams!
God gave the realm, God gives the Light—
    How sweet, how bright,
      It beams!

That torch is Love, whose lucent ray
    Slays all things cruel and unclean !
No shadow clouds it night or day,
While sun and moon keep equal sway,
    Calm and serene.
God gives this torch with heaven-fed ray
    To light thy way,
        O Queen !

Let this thy guide and sceptre be,
    And power and peace may still be thine,
All mortal men shall bend the knee,
All men revere, in thine and thee,
    The Law Divine.
Blest shall thy mighty Empire be,
While o'er the world, from sea to sea,
The sunlight of thy Jubilee
    Shall shine !

"ANNIE;"

OR, THE WAIF'S JUBILEE.

"The magistrate asked her what she had to say for herself.
"Only this, sir," she replied, "*I was a gentleman's daughter once.*"
—Police Report.

> "*Annie! Annie!*"
> *Hark, it is Father's call!*
> *See, he is coming! Run*
> *To meet him, little one,*
>   *In the golden evenfall.*
> *Yonder down the lane*
> *His voice calls clear:*
> "*Annie!*" *he cries again—*
> *Run down and meet him, dear!*
> *The long day's toil is done,*
>   *The hour of rest has come—*
> *Haste to him, little one—*
> *Ride on his shoulder home!*

. . . What voice is this she hears across the storm,
The haggard Waif who stands with dripping form
   Shivering beneath the lamps of the dark street?
With slant moist beams upon the Rain's black walls
The dreary gaslight falls,
   And all around the wings o' the Tempest beat!
O hark! O hark!
The voice calls clear i' the dark—
   She hears—she moans—and moaning wanders on :
A mist before her eyes,
A stone in her heart, she flies
   Into the rainy darkness, and is gone!

What a night! strong and blind
Down the street swoops the Wind,
*   Falls breathless, then moans!*
While again and again
Like a spirit in pain,
*   On the black slippery stones*
*   Sobs the Rain! . . .*

"Annie! Annie!"
*   Hark, it is Father's call!*
See, he is coming! Run
To meet him, little one,
*   In the golden evenfall!*

. . . Out from the darkness she hath crept once more,
   That strange voice ringing hollow over all;
Close to the theatre's great lighted door,
Where smiling ladies, while the raindrops pour,
   Wait for their carriages, and linkmen bawl.
She pauses watching, while they laugh and pass,
Tripping across the pavement 'neath the gas,
Then rattling home. Home? Ah, what home hath *she*,
   Who once was bright and glad as any there?
Fifty years old, this is her Jubilee!
And round her Life is like an angry Sea
   Breaking to ululations of despair!

Who hath not seen her, on dark nights of rain,
   Or when the Moon is chill on the chill street,
Creeping from shade to shade in grief and pain,
Showing her painted cheeks for man's disdain,
   And wrapt in woe as in a winding sheet?
Sin hath so stain'd it none may recognise
   The face that once was innocent and fair,
And hollow rings are round the hungry eyes,
   And shocks of grey replace the golden hair.

And all her chance is, when the drink makes blind
The foulest and the meanest of mankind,
To hide her stains and face a hideous mirth,
　　And gain her body's food the old foul way—
Ah, loathsome dead sea fruit that eats like earth,
　　Her mouth is foul with it both night and day!
So that corruption and the stench of Death
Consume her body and pollute her breath,
And all the world she looks upon appears
A dismal charnel-house of lust and tears!
Sick of the horror that corrupts the flesh,
Tangled in vice as in a spider's mesh,
Scenting the lazar-house, in soul's despair,
She sees the gin shop's bloodshot eyeballs glare,
And creepeth in, the feverish drug to drain
That blots the sense and blinds the aching brain;
And then with feeble form and faltering feet
Again she steals into the midnight street,
Seeks for her prey, and woefully takes flight
To join her spectral sisters of the Night!

　　　　What a Night! fierce and blind!
　　　　Down the street swoops the Wind!
　　　　How it moans! how it groans!
　　　　While again and again
　　　　Like a spirit in pain,
　　　　　On the black slippery stones
　　　　　　Sobs the Rain!
　　　　See! like ghosts to and fro
　　　　　Living forms swiftly pass,
　　　　With their shadows below
　　　　　In the gleam of the gas;
　　　　And the swells, wrapt up warm,
　　　　　With their weeds blazing bright,
　　　　Hurry home thro' the Storm . . .
　　　　　It's a Hell of a Night!

Hell ? She is *in* it, and these shapes she sees,
    While crawling on, are hateful and accurst !
Light laughter of light lips, mad images
    Of dainty creatures delicately nurst,
Cries of the revel, blackness, and the gleam
Of ghastly lights, are blended in her dream
Of Hell that lives and is, the Hell she knows,
With all its mockery of human woes !
Darkly, as in a glass, she seeth plain
The vision of dead days that live again :
The house, beyond these streets, where she was born ;
    The father's face in death ; the hungry home ;
The fight for bread ; the hungry and forlorn
    Cry for a help and guide that would not come ;
The glimmer of glad halls, the forms therein
    Beck'ning and laughing till she joined their mirth ;
Then, pleasures sultry with the sense of sin,
    And those foul dead sea fruits that taste of earth ;
Then, blackness of disease and utter shame,
And all Hell's infamies without a name !
Then, all the bloom of sense and spirit fled,
The slow descent to midnight gulfs of dread
Like *this* she sees !—Then, in a wretched room
Deep mid the City's sunless heart of gloom,
Another life awakening 'neath her heart,
A sickly babe with crying lips apart
Moaning for food !—and into Hell she creeps
    Once more to feed it, haunting the black street,—
Yea, in the garret where her infant sleeps
    Hell's hideous rites are done, that it may eat !
Then, Death once more ! The sickly life at rest ;
    The child's light coffin that a child might bear ;
The mother's hunger tearing at her breast,
    And only Drink to drown the soul's despair.
She sees it all, on this her Jubilee,
    While the Night moans, and the sick Hell-lights
        gleam . . .

O God! O Motherhood! Can these things be,
  And men still say that Hell is but a dream?

       " Annie! Annie!"
     What voice is this that cries,
     Amid the lights of Hell,
    Where these live shadows dwell
     Under the rain-rent skies? . . .
    What a night! All one hears
     Is the torrent of tears
      On a World plung'd in pain ;
    All one sees is the swarm
     Of dim waifs in the Storm,
    Flitting hither and thither,
     (O God, who knows whither?)
      Like ghosts, thro' the Rain!

. . . *Annie!* . . .
  She hears the voice, ev'n while she crawls
    'Neath the black arches on the riverside,
Then moaning low upon her face she falls . . .
Annie! . . . She stirs, and listens as it calls,
    With eyes that open wide.
Lost there to Man, dead to the Storm and Strife,
    She lies and keeps her Jubilee till morn,.
O'er her, a heap of rags, the waves of Life
    Wash weary and forlorn . . .
Is all, then, done? Nay, from the depths of Night
That voice still cries, and dimly gleams a Light . . .
" *Annie!* "—She listens—Thro' the Tempest wild
    One cometh softly—she can *see* him come!—
" *Father! I'm Annie! I'm your little child!* "
    And Father lifts her up, to bear her Home!

L'ENVOI TO THE PRECEDING POEM.

I.

COURAGE, and face the strife of Humankind
    In patience, O my brother:
We come from the eternal Night to find,
    And not to lose, each other!

Think'st thou thy God hath toil'd thro' endless Time
    With ceaseless strong endeavour,
To fashion these and thee from ooze and slime,
    Then blot his work for ever?

Age after age hath roll'd in billowy strife
    On the eternal Ocean,
Bearing us hither to these sands of Life
    With sure and steadfast motion.

Dead? Nought that lives can die. We live, and see!
    So hush thy foolish grieving:
This Universe was made that thou might'st be
    Incarnate, self-perceiving.

Still thine own Soul, if thou would'st still the strife
    Of phantoms round thee flying;
Remember that the paradox of Life
    Is Death, the Life undying.

II.

How? *Thou* be saved, and one of these be lost?
    The least of these be spent, and thou soar free?
Nay! for these things are *thou*—these tempest-tost
    Waves of the darkness are but forms of thee.

Shall these be cast away? Then rest thou sure
    No hopes abide for thee if none for these.
Would'st thou be heal'd? Then hast thou these to cure;
    Thine is their shame, their foulness, their disease.

By these, thy shadows, shalt thou rise or fall;
    Thro' these and thee, God reigns, or rests down-trod;
Let Him but lose but one, He loses all,
    And losing all, He too is lost, ev'n God.

These shapes are only images of thee,
    Nay, very God is thou and all things thine:
Thou art the Eye with which Eternity
    Surveys itself, and knows itself Divine!

PHERSON'S WOOING.

A BAGPIPE BALLAD, AFTER MACHOMER.

Note.—In this Homeric ballad of modern marriage by capture in the Scottish Highlands, several customs are described which are not even yet altogether extinct,—for example, the old Highland custom of midnight courtship in the lady's chamber, described in Pherson's relation of his nocturnal visits to Meg Nicraonail. For the rest, I myself have personal knowledge of a rape of the kind celebrated in the poem. The results, however, were unfortunate, for although the bold lover succeeded in bearing the bride the prescribed distance from her father's door, he eventually died of the injuries inflicted by her kinsmen. R. B.

(Tune up, Pipers!)

With red, unshear'd
Beard,
Fiery eyes by foemen fear'd,
Form gigantic famed in story,
Standing on the bleak and wide
Mountain side,
Cried
Neil Macpherson of Tobermory.

(Foot and elbow, now, together!)

"Pherson is my name!" (the throngs
Shriek'd in approbation)
"Tuncan Pherson of the Songs
Wass my blood-relation!
Many a Pherson great and small
Has been counted clever,
And the Phersons, one and all,
Are goot men, whatever!
Yonder up the heathery strath
Dwells sweet Meg Nicraonail,*

---

* Note.—Pronounce *Nicronnell*. *MacRaonail*, in Gaelic, the *son* of Raonail; *NicRaonail*, the *daughter* of Raonail.

Fairest lassie from Cape Wrath
  Southward to Strath Connell ;
Breastit like the swan so light,
  Lintwhite-lockit Meg is,
Eyes like stars, and limbs as white
  As a pullet's egg is !
Many a day, ochone a rie,
  I have woo't this person,
On my naked bended knee
Pray'd and pleaded she would be
  Bride and wife of Pherson.
Sirs, she longs to be my bride,
  Does this dainty leddy,
But her kinsmen, tamn their pride !
Say the knot shall ne'er be tied
  Tho' herself is ready !
Shall I bear their scoff and scorn,
  Leave her and forsake her ?
Or, between the mirk and morn,
  Mother-naked take her ?
I have call'd you here to speak—
  Speak, then, now or never ! "
Loud as thunder rose the shriek :
  " Take her, Neil, whatever ! "

     (Skirl!)

Tall, gigantic,
Fierce and frantic,
  Tossing down his bonnet,
Gray Shon Alastair MacCall
Cried, " We're with you, one and all,—
  There's my fist upon it !
Send the message town the glen,
Gather all your fighting men,
  Lads of kilt and plaidie,
Teach the Raonails (tamn their clan !)

F

How to treat a shentleman
  When he coorts a leddy !"

    (Step tune, cannily!)

By the waters of the Shiel
  To the ocean booming,
Braes of heather 'neath their heel,
Hills of heather stiff to speel *
  Up behind them looming,
Gather'd Pherson's friends and kin,
  Men of thew and sinew,
Crying, " 'Tis yoursel' shall win !
Put some whiskey in your skin !
  Show the stuff that's in you !"
Up along the lonely pass,
  By the torrent's water,
Stood the dwelling of the lass,
  Shon Macraonail's daughter ;
And the Raonails from afar
  Saw with trepidation
(Knowing it portended war)
  Pherson's preparation.

    (Pipers, still cannily!)

There's a Highland law, as old
  As the great MacMoses,
Says—if any wooer bold
Dares, when flocks are in the fold,
  And the house reposes,
In his arms a maid to seize
  Spite her kin's prevention
(Duly notifying these,
  First, of his intention),

---

    * Climb.

He the lassie shall possess,
    After due persistence,—
But his failure or success
    Shall be judged *by distance* :
If beyond her father's door
Full five hundred yards or more
    He his prize can carry,
Spite of stones and spite of blows,
Cracking crown or bloody nose,
    He the maid may marry!
Nay, her kinsmen, when 'tis done,
    Shall admit politely
That the bride is fairly won,
    Ta'en and captured rightly ;
Casting hate and strife away,
    All, with smiling faces,
Shall 'mid floods of usquebae *
    Bless that pair's embraces!

That's the custom! but it needs
    One of resolution,
Train'd in strength of doughty deeds,
    For its execution!
Such was Pherson! such were those
    Thronging round the giant!
Tiptoe, like the cock that crows
Battle-challenge to his foes,
    Stood red Neil, defiant!
" Long the lass has let me woo
    In the Hieland fashion—
[Och, she is a dainty doo,†
    Full of tender passion !]
Many a night outside her bed

---

* Mountain dew, or whiskey.   † Dove.

I my shaggy limbs have spread,
 When no een have seen us,
Underneath the blankets she,
Keeking out and kissing me,
 But—the claise between us!
While her folk were snoring sound,
Fondly clasping arms around
 This most charming person,
I of kisses took my fill;
But a kiss, sirs, cannot still
 Love in Neil Macpherson!
I will seize her, by my saul,
 And resign her never!"
Loud as thunder rose the call
From the throats of one and all,
 "Take her, Neil, whatever!"

  (*Reel time, Pipers!*)

Down Strathconnell ran the cry
 Ringing out a warning:
"Neil the Pherson means to try
Theft and capture, tho' he die,
 'Twixt the mirk and morning!"
Thick as bees round honied bykes
 Clansmen ring'd the lady,—
" Let him come as soon 's he likes!
 Gott, he'll find us ready!"
Round the fire their cups they drained,
 Arm'd and breathing slaughter,
While the sun with crimson stained
 Mountain, moor, and water.
Trembling in the inner room
 Lay the longing Maiden,
Blushing like a rose in bloom,
 Listening terror-laden . . .
Pass'd the dusky Eventide,
 Stars above grew thicker,

Faster round the ingleside
    Went the fiery liquor!
Crouching on their cutty seats *
    Dame and granddame listened,
While as red as flaming peats
    Angry faces glisten'd.
" Tamn the Pherson and his kin!
    Aal his sheneration!
If he dares to enter in,
    There'll be potheration! "
Lying in the inner room
    Meg could hear them screaming,
Smell the fiery whiskey-fume
    From the circle steaming!

      (*Now softly, Pipers!*)

Darker, stiller grew the night,
    Hour by hour departed,—
Laughing louder in delight
Raonail's kinsmen arm'd for fight
    Grew more valiant-hearted.
" Tamn the Pherson! In his bed
    Full of fear he's lying!
Deil a step this way he'll tread! "
    Meg could hear them crying . . .
Fainter soon the revel rung,
    Sleepy eyes were closing,
One by one the clansmen hung
    Heavy noddles, dozing . . .
Meg arose, and at the door,
    In her sark,† half-frozen,
Listen'd! Silence! Then a snore!
    Then an answering dozen!

---

    * Low stools.   † Nightgown.

Then her lighted lamp she took,
  Full of trepidation,
Set it in her window-nook—
  Signal for invasion!
[Even so sweet Hero gave
  Warning to her wooer,
Guiding him across the wave
  Mother-naked to her!]
Back to bed the maiden flies,
  List'ning (sly young person!)
Till, like lightning from the skies,
On the clansmen's sleepy eyes
  Breaks the form of Pherson!!

(*Skirl, Pipers, Skirl!*)

Up they sprang and sought their brands,
  Near them idly lying,
Through their ranks with mighty hands
  Pherson now was flying.
Soon he reach'd the chamber dark,
Seized the lassie in her sark;
  Loud she shriek'd (but kissed him!)
Bore her crying to the door,
Faced the frantic clan, once more
  Ready to resist him!
As a torrent tears amain
  Over rocks and boulders,
While the blows fell down like rain
  On his sinewy shoulders,
Neil the Pherson all alone
  Swept thro' men and women—
Thick as ninepins overthrown
  Fell the kilted foemen!
Bleeding wounds upon his brow,
  Blood his features staining,
On he bears the prize, and—wow!
  He the door is gaining!

After him the Raonails stream,
    Striking, cursing, chasing,—
Maggie still pretends to scream,
    His strong neck embracing!
Out into the night he flies,
    Panting, struggling, springing,
Bearing off the bonnie prize,
    Kissing, cuddling, clinging!
Warm'd by kisses such as those
    From Macraonail's daughter,
Heedless of the raining blows,
Pherson, followed by his foes,
    Nears the running water!
There, five hundred yards and more
From Macraonail's open door,
    Pherson's friends are glaring—
Wild their "hooch!" to heaven rings,
As the riever thither springs,
    His white burthen bearing.
Swift into the nut-brown stream,
    Round his middle gushing,
Strides he, while with angry scream
    Come the Raonails rushing!
Raonails now on Phersons clash,
    Shrieking and opposing!
Spluttersmash and splatterdash!
In the shallow pools they splash,
    Like two wrestlers closing!
Long they fight and twist and turn,
    But the race is over—
Side by side beyond the burn
    Sit the lass and lover! (*Hooch!*)
Pherson, wounded from the fray,
Wiping clots of blood away,
    Laughing, takes his plaidie,
Wraps it like a blanket warm

Round the dripping, drooping form
    Of his dainty lady.
Mouth to mouth and breast to breast
    Now they cling in passion,
Pherson's very soul is blest
    Past anticipation—
Then with crow of joy and pride
    He his prize upraises,
Bears her down the mountain side,
While the Dawning sleepy-eyed
    O'er the hill-tops gazes!

(Slow time, toe and heel, softly, softly!)

So Macraonail's child was won
    By the law of thieving!
So the doughty deed was done
By the Pherson, Pherson's son,
    Valiant past believing!
That day week the feast was spread
    When the sun sank rosy;
While the holy rites were said,
Lasses on the bridal bed
    Spread the blankets (cosy!)
Thronging in the Raonails ran,
    With good whiskey laden—
" Pherson, you're a shentleman,
    And deserfe the maiden! "
Of the mighty midnight fray
    Each betrayed some token—
Here a lug* clean sliced away,
    There a strong arm broken;
One came hirpling† on a staff,
    Smiling at disaster,
T'other's nose, cut clean in half,
    Clung to sticking plaster!

* Ear.   † Limping.

But the Phersons with the same
  Battle-signs were sprinkled—
Some were bandaged, most were lame ;
Of MacCall's two eyes of flame
  Only one now twinkled !
With a patch on either eye,
  Features stain'd with slaughter,
Pherson sat triumphant, by
  Raonail's dainty daughter . . .
While they gather in accord
Ranging round the festal board
  Broken heads and noses,
Grim Shon Alastair MacCall,
Patch'd and broken from the brawl,
  Pherson's health proposes :
" Here's the Pherson and his clan !
Sirs, he iss the lad who can
  Gife and take a threshing !
Health to all who fought that night !
By my saul, it was a fight
  Pleasant and refreshing ! "
Hand grips hand, and all around
  Smile with plaster'd faces,
Pipers play, and at the sound,
While the kilted dancers bound,
  Neil his bride embraces.
" Pherson is my name ! " he cries,
  " Noble is my clan, sirs !
Tamn the rascal who denies
  I'm a shentleman, sirs ! "
" Pherson ! Pherson ! " rings the call
From the throats of great and small,
  " Hooch, but he is clever ! "
" Here's to Pherson and the wife ! "
" Take her, Pherson—all her life
  She is yours, whatever ! "

THE BALLAD OF MAGELLAN.*

(Spoken in the Person of one of his Lieutenants,
dying at Home, Years after the Wonderful Voyage
was over.)

Send no shaven monks to shrive me, close the doors
    against their cries ;
Liars all ! ay, rogues and liars, like the Father of all lies ;
Nay, but open wide the casement, once more let me feast
    my gaze
On the glittering signs of Heaven, on the mighty Ocean-
    ways !

Who's that knocking ? Fra Ramiro ? Left his wine-cup
    and arm-chair,
Come again with book and ointment, to anoint me and
    prepare ?
Sacremento !—send him packing, with his comrades
    shaven-crown'd :
Liars all ! and prince of liars is their Pope ! The world
    is round !

See, the Ocean ! like quicksilver, throbbing in the starry
    light !
See the stars and constellations, strangely, mystically
    bright !
Ah, but there, beyond our vision, other stars look brightly
    down,
Other stars, and high among them, great Magellan's
    starry crown !

---

  * Magellan was the first man to circumnavigate the earth, and
thus to establish the scientific theory that the world was a globe.

O Magellan! Lord and Master!—mighty soul no Pope
    could tame!
On the seas and on the heavens you have left your radiant
    name;
Brightly shall it burn for ever, o'er the waters without
    bound,
Proving Pope and Priests still liars, while the sun-kist
    world is round.

Let the cowls at Salamanca cluster thick as rook and
    daw!
Let the Pope with right hand palsied clutch his thunder-
    bolts of straw!
Heaven and Ocean, here and yonder, put their feeble
    deeds to shame;
Earth is round, and high above it shines Magellan's starry
    name!

Have you vanish'd, O my Master? O my Captain, King
    of men,
Shall I never more behold you standing at the mast
    again,
Eagle-eyed, and stern and silent, never sleeping or at
    rest,
Pallid as a man of marble, ever looking to the west?

As I lie and watch the heavens, once again I seem to be
Out upon the waste of waters, sailing on from sea to
    sea. . . .
Hark! what's that?—the monks intoning in the chapel
    close at hand?
Nay, I hear but sea-birds screaming, round dark capes of
    lonely land!

Out upon the still equator, on a sea without a breath,
Burning, blistering in the sunlight, we are tossing sick to
    death;

Every night the sun sinks crimson on the water's endless
    swell,
Every dawn he rises burning, fiery as the flames of Hell.

Seventy days our five brave vessels welter in the watery
    glare,
O'er the bulwarks hang the seamen panting open-mouth'd
    for air ;
On the " Trinitie " Magellan watches in a fierce unrest,
Never doubting, or despairing, ever looking to the west.

Then at last with fire and thunder open cracks the sultry
    sky,
While the surging seas roll under, swift before the blast
    we fly,
Westward, ever westward, plunging, while the waters
    wash and wail ;
Nights and days drift past in darkness while we sail,
    and sail, and sail.

Then the Tempest, like an eagle by a thunderbolt struck
    dead,
With one last wild flap of pinions, droppeth spent and
    bloody-red,
Purpling Heaven and Ocean lieth on the dark horizon's
    brink,
While upon the decks we gather silently, and watch him
    sink.

Troublously the Ocean labours in a last surcease of pain,
While a soft breath blowing westward wafts us softly
    on the main,—-
Nearer to the edge of darkness where the flat earth ends,
    men swear,
Where the dark abysses open, gulf on gulf of empty air !

Creeping silently our vessels enter wastes of wondrous
  weed,
Slimy growth that clings around them, tangle growing
  purple seed,
Staining all the waste of waters, making isles of floating
  black,
While the seamen, pointing fingers, shrink in dread, and
  cry, " Turn back ! "

On the " Trinitie " Magellan stands and looks with fear-
  less eyes—
" Fools, the world is round ! " he answers, " onward still
  our pathway lies ;
Though the gulfs of Hell yawn'd yonder, though the
  Earth were ended there,
I would venture boldly forward, facing Death and Death's
  despair."

On their knees they kneel unto him, cross themselves and
  shriek afraid,
Pallid as a man of marble stands the Captain undismayed,
Claps on sail and leads us onward, while the ships crawl
  in his track,
Slowly, scarcely moving, trailing monstrous weeds that
  hold them back.

On each vessel's prow a seaman stands and casts the
  sounding-lead,
In the cage high up the foremast gather watchers sick
  with dread.
Calmly on the poop Magellan marks the heavens and
  marks the sea,
Darkness round and darkness o'er him, closing round the
  " Trinitie."

Days and nights of deeper darkness follow—then there
    comes the cry,
" He is mad—Death waits before us—turn the ships and
    let us fly ! "
Storm of mutinous anger gathers round the Captain stern
    and true,
Near the foremast, fiercely glaring, flash the faces of the
    crew.

One there is, a savage seaman, gnashing teeth and waving
    hands,
Strides with curses to the Captain where with folded arms
    he stands,—
"Turn, thou madman, turn!" he shrieketh. Scarcely
    hath he spoke the word,
Ere a bleeding log he falleth, slaughter'd by the Leader's
    sword !

" Fools and cowards ! " cries Magellan, spurning him with
    arméd heel,
" If another dreams of flying, let him speak—and taste
    my steel ! "
Like caged tigers when the Tamer enters calmly, shrink
    the band,
While the Master strides among them, cloth'd in mail and
    sword in hand.

O Magellan ! Lord and Leader !—only He whose fingers
    frame
Twisted thews of pard or panther, knot them round their
    hearts of flame,
Light the emeralds burning brightly in their eyeballs as
    they roll,
Could have made that mightier marvel, thine inexorable
    Soul !

Onward, ever on, we falter—till there comes a dawn of
    day
Creeping ghostly up behind us, mirror'd faintly far away,
While across the sea to starboard loometh strangely land
    · or cloud—
" Land to starboard ! " cries Magellan—" Land ! " the
    seamen call aloud.

Southward steering creep the vessels, while the lights of
    morning grow ;
Fades the land, while in our faces chilly fog and vapour
    blow ;
Colder grows the air, and clinging round the masts and
    stiffening sails
Freezes into crystal dewdrops, into hanging icicles !

Suddenly arise before us, phantom-wise, as in eclipse,
Icebergs drifting on the Ocean like innumerable ships—
In the light they flash prismatic as among their throng
    we creep,
Crashing down to overwhelm us, thundering to the
    thund'rous Deep !

Towering ghostly and gigantic, 'midst the steam of their
    own breath,
Moving northward in procession in their snowy shrouds
    of Death,
Rise the bergs, now overtoppling like great torrents in
    the air,
While along their crumbling edges slips the seal and
    steals the bear.

With the frost upon his armour, like a skeleton of steel,
Stands the Master, waiting, watching, clad in cold from
    head to heel ;

Loud his voice rings through the vapours, ordering all
and leading on,
Till the bergs, before his finger, fall back ghostlike, and
are gone!

Once again before our vision sparkles Ocean wide and
free,
With the sun's red ball of crimson resting on the rim of
sea;—
" Lo, the sun! " he laughs exulting—" still he beckons
far away—
Earth is round, and on its circle evermore we chase the
Day! "

As he speaks the sunset blackens.   Twilight trembles
through the skies
For a moment—then the heavens open all their starry
eyes!
Suddenly strange Constellations flash from out the fields
of blue—
Not a star that we remember, not a splendour priestcraft
knew!

Sinking on his knee, Magellan prays: " Now glory be to
God!
To the Christ who led us forward on His wondrous
watery road!
See, the heavens give attestation that our search shall
yet be crowned,
Proving Pope and Priests are liars, and the sun-kist world
is round! "

Sparkling ruby-ray'd and golden round the dusky neck
of Night
Hangs a jewell'd Constellation, strangely, mystically
bright—

Pointing at it cries the Master, " By the God we all
    adore,
It shall bear *my* name, MAGELLAN !" and it bears it,
    evermore.

Storms arising sweep us onward, but each night our
    courage grows,
Newer portals of the Heaven seem to open and unclose,
Showing in the blue abysm vistas luminously strange,
Sphere on sphere, and far beyond them fainter lights that
    sparkle and change !

Presently once more we falter among pools of drifting
    scum,
Weed and tangle—o'er the blackness curious sea-birds go
    and come—
While to southward looms a darkness, as of land or
    gathering cloud,
Northward too, another darkness, and a sound of breakers
    loud.

Once again they call in terror, " Turn again, for Death is
    near ! "
Once again he quells their tumult, smiting till they
    crouch in fear.
On with darkness closing round them, land or cloud, our
    fleet is led,
Fighting tides that sweep them backward, flowing from
    some gulf of dread.

Next the Vision ! next the Morning, after rayless nights
    and days,
Twinkling on a great calm Ocean stretching far as eye
    can gaze,—
Newer heavens and newer waters, solitary and profound,
Rise before us, while behind us Day arises crimson-
    crown'd !

Turning, we behold the shadows of the straits through
　　which we sped,
Then again our eyes look forward where the windless
　　waters spread ;
Overhead the sun rolls golden, moving westward through
　　the blue,
Reddens down the far-off heavens, beckons bright, and
　　we pursue.

On that vast and tranquil Ocean, folding wings the strong
　　winds dwell,
Sleeping softly or just stirring to the water's tranquil
　　swell,
Peaceful as the fields of heaven where the stars like
　　bright flocks feed,—
So that many dream they wander thro' the azure Heaven
　　indeed !

Then Magellan, from its scabbard drawing forth his
　　shining sword,
Grasps the blade, and downward bending, dips the bright
　　hilt overboard—
" By the holy Cross's likeness, mirror'd in this hilt ! "
　　cries he,
" Be this Ocean called Pacific, since it sleeps eternallie ! "

Pastured with a calm eternal, drawing down the clouds
　　in dew,
Sighing low with soft pulsations, darkly, mystically blue,
Lies that long untrodden Ocean, while for months we sail
　　it o'er ;
Ever dawns the sun behind us, ever swiftly sets before.

But like devils out of Tophet, as we sail with God for
　　Guide,
Rise the spectres, Thirst and Hunger, hollow-cheek'd and
　　cruel-eyed ;

Fierce and famish'd creep the seamen, while the tongues
    between their teeth
Loll like tongues of hounds for water, dry as dust and
    black with death.

Many fall and die blaspheming; "Give us food!" the
    living call—
Pallid as a man of marble stands the Master gaunt and
    tall,
Hunger fierce within him also, and his parch'd lips prest
    in pain,
But a mightier thirst and hunger burning in his heart
    and brain !

Black decks blistering in the sunlight, sails and cordage
    dry as clay,
Crawl the ships on those still Waters night by night and
    day by day ;
Then the rain comes, and we lap it as upon the decks it
    flows—
"Spread a sail!" calls out the Master, and we catch it ere
    it goes.

Now and then a lonely sea-bird hovers far away, and we
Crouch with hungry eyes and watch it fluttering closer
    o'er the sea,
Curse it if it flies beyond us, shoot it if it cometh nigh,
Share the flesh and blood among us, underneath the
    Captain's eye.

Sometimes famished unto madness, fierce as wolves that
    shriek in strife,
One man springs upon another, stabs him with the
    murderous knife ;

Then the Master, stalking forward where the murderer
 shrinks in dread,
Bids him kneel, and as he kneeleth cleaves him down, and
 leaves him dead.

O Magellan! mighty Eagle, circling sunward lost in light,
Wafting wings of power and striking meaner things that
 cross thy flight,
God to such as thee gives never lambkin's love or dove's
 desire—
Nay, but eyes that scatter terror from a ruthless heart of
 fire!

Give me wine. My pulses falter. . . So! . . . . Confusion
 to the cowls!
They who hooted at my Eagle, eyes of bats and heads of
 owls!
Throw the casement open wider! There is something yet
 to tell—
How we came at last to waters where the naked islesmen
 dwell.

Isles of wonder, fringed with coral, ring'd with shallows
 turquoise-blue,
Where bright fish and crimson monsters flash'd their
 jewell'd lights and flew,
Steeps of palm that rose to heaven out of purple depths
 of sea,
While upon their sunlit summits stirr'd the tufted coca-
 tree—

Isles of cinnabar and spices, where soft airs for ever creep,
Scenting Ocean all around them with strange odours soft
 as sleep—

Isles about whose promontories danced the black man's
    light canoe,
Isles where dark-eyed women beckon'd, perfumed like the
    breath they drew.

Drunken with the sight we landed, rush'd into the scented
    glades,
Treading down the scented branches, seized the struggling
    savage maids.
Ah, the orgy! Still it sickens!—blood of men bestrewed
    our path,
Till the islesmen rose against us, thick as vultures, shriek-
    ing wrath.

Then, the sequel! Nay, I know not how the damnèd
    deed could be—
By some islesman's poisoned arrow or some Spaniard's
    treacherie;
But one evening as we struggled fighting to our boats on
    shore,
In the shallows fell the Captain, foully slain, and rose no
    more!

O Magellan! O my Master! O my Captain, King of men!
Was it fit thou so shouldst perish, though thy work was
    over then?
Foully slain by foe or comrade, butcher'd like a common
    thing,
Thou whose eagle flight had circled Earth upon undaunted
    wing!

Nay, but then my King had conquered! Earth and Ocean
    to his sight
Open'd had their wondrous visions, shaming centuries of
    night:

Nay, but even the shining Heavens kept the record of his
    fame—
Earth was round, and high above it shone Magellan's
    starry name!

How our wondrous voyage ended?   Nay, I know not,—
    all was done ;
Lying in my ship I sickened, moaning, hidden from the
    sun.
Yea ! the vessels drifted onward till they came to isles of
    calm,
Where some savage monarch hail'd them, standing under-
    neath a palm.

How the wanderers took these islands tributary to our
    King,
Show'd the Cross, baptized the monarch, homeward crept
    on weary wing ?
Pshaw, 'tis nothing !   All was over ! *He* had staked his
    soul and gained,
They but reaped the Master's sowing, they but crawl'd
    where he had reigned !

Hark ? what sound is that ?   The chiming of the dreary
    vesper bell ?
Nay, I hear but Ocean sighing, feel the waters heave and
    swell.
Earth is round, but sailing sunward with my Master still
    I fare—
Other Heavens his ship is searching,—and I go to seek
    him *there* !

THE BURIAL OF PARNELL.

(Spoken in the Person of one of his Followers).

" We come to bury Cæsar, not to praise him."

1.

WE come to bury Cæsar, not
   To praise him!—yet our eyes
Grow dim above the holy spot
   Where our dead Monarch lies;
The hungry millions, weeping too,
   Mourn their lost Lord and Friend,
While here we stand, the faithful few
   Who loved him till the end!

2.

Cæsar lies dead!—yea, Cæsar! Tho'
   His brows were never crown'd,
He reigned, until the assassin's blow
   First struck him to the ground;
He walk'd imperial in command,
   While angry factions raved—
Sad Cæsar of the woeful Land
   Which he redeemed and saved!

3.

Cæsar is dead!—no golden throne
   Or purple robes sought he,
But led, in darkness and alone,
   Legions that would be free;
His armies were the famish'd throng
   That rose and march'd by night,
A living Host that swept along
   To some great Land of Light!

4.

The dim Light grows, the Dawn is nigh!
   But he who led us on,
Who held the fiery Cross on high
   Thro' the long night, is gone!
Full at his heart the cowards smote
   With many a trait'rous thrust,
While Falsehood fasten'd on his throat
   And dragg'd him to the dust! . . .

5.

Ev'n as a Lion fixing eyes
   On something far away,
He stood alone 'neath sunless skies
   On his great triumph-day;
Then, while he march'd the battle-place,
   His jackals gather'd in . . .
And *now*? The things which fear'd his face
   Fight for the Lion's skin!

6.

What one of these shall put it on?
   Thou, weakest of the weak,
Who, when thy Lord lay woe-begone,
   First kiss'd, then smote, his cheek?
Or *thou*, who mock'd him in his fall
   With foul and impious jest?
Or *thou*, the basest of them all,
   Who gnaw'd the bleeding breast?

7.

Jackals and cowards, mourn elsewhere!
   Not near the mighty Dead!
Your breath pollutes the holy air
   Around a Martyr's bed.

Go ! fatten with the Scribes and Priests
   Who led your foul array,
Or crouch, with all the timorous beasts
   Who follow'd him for prey !

8.

Who slew this Man ? The cruel Foe
   That stab'd our Erin first ;
Then Brutus, loth to strike the blow ;
   Then Casca, the accurst ;
Then freedmen by his hands unbound,
   And slaves his hands had fed,
Joining the throng that ring'd him round,
   Stoned him till he was dead!

9.

Lo, where the English Brutus stands,
   With white and reverend hair,
Bloodstains upon the wrinkled hands
   He calmly folds in prayer ;
Facing all ways beneath the sky,
   Strong still, tho' worn and wan,
This Brutus is (so all men cry)
   "An honourable man " !

10.

Casca and Cassius haggard-eyed,
   Their gaze on Brutus' face,
Say, "Surely Cæsar had not died
   If *thou* had given him grace ! "
O thrice-bound Freeman, in whose name
   They proved this dead Man base,
Still keep from unbelief and shame
   Thy Marriage Market-place !

11.

There, where the White Slave, Woman, stands,
    Wearing her gyves of gold,
Soothe with the ointment of the creeds
    The body ere 'tis sold ;
Preach the high Law of Purity,
    Find out all stains and slurs,
And keep the great Slave-market free
    To righteous purchasers!

12.

But, Brutus, thou who conjurest
    In Freedom's sacred name,
Back from this grave, mar not this rest,
    Breathe not this Martyr's name!
Priests on thy left hand and thy right,
    Stand up and prate of God,
While he thou didst betray and smite
    Lies dead beneath the sod!

13.

Still, where thou standest, bending o'er
    Thy head, and blessing thee,
Broods the pale Babylonian Whore
    They name " Morality " :
Making a noble spirit blind
    With her polluting breath,
She found the means Hate could not find,
    And plann'd the deed of Death !

14.

Who slew this man ? Thou, Christian Land,
    Who sendest o'er the foam
Mammon and Murther hand in hand
    To shame the Christ at home!

The Christ? His painted Image, nurst
 By knaves who cast on men
The curse of Priestcraft—last and worst,
 The Priestcraft of the Pen!

15.

Not till our King lay bleeding there,
 Crept forth with cruel eyne
The venom'd things which make their lair
 Beneath the Seven-Hill'd Shrine:
Then, in the name of him they priced,
 Degraded, and betrayed,
They poisoned, these false priests of Christ,
 The wounds a Judas made!

16.

We come to bury, not to praise
 Our Cæsar—yet his knell
Joins with the cry of wrath we raise
 'Gainst those thro' whom he fell!
While Freemen pass from hand to hand
 The Fiery Cross he waved,
His fame shall lighten thro' the Land
 Which he redeemed and saved!

TOM DUNSTAN; OR, THE POLITICIAN.

" How long, O Lord, how long ? "

1.

Now poor Tom Dunstan's cold,
   All life's grown duller ;
There's a blight on young and old,
And our talk has lost its bold
   Red-republican colour !
Poor Tom was crippled and thin,
   But Lord, if you'd seen his face,
When, sick of the country's sin,
With bang of the fist, and chin
   Stuck out, he argued the case !
He prophesied men should be free !
   And the money-bags be bled !
" She's coming, she's coming ! " said he ;
" Courage, boys ! wait and see !
   Freedom's ahead ! "

2.

Cross-leg'd on the board we sat,
   Like spiders spinning,
Stitching and sweating, while fat
Old Moses, with eyes like a cat,
   Sat greasily grinning ;
And here Tom said his say,
   And prophesied Tyranny's death ;
And the tallow burned all day,
And we stitch'd and stitch'd away
   In the thick smoke of our breath.

Poor worn-out slops were we,
  With hearts as heavy as lead ;
But "Patience! she's coming!" said he ;
" Courage, boys! wait and see!
  Freedom's ahead ! "

3.

And at night, when we took here
  The rest allowed to us,
The Paper came, with the beer,
And Tom read, sharp and clear,
  The news out loud to us ;
Then, warm with the "half and half,"
  He'd go it, hammer and claws !
And Lord, how we used to laugh
To hear him smother with chaff
  The Snobs who make the laws !
And it made us breathe more free
  To hearken to what he said—
"She's coming! she's coming!" said he ;
" Courage, boys! wait and see!
  Freedom's ahead ! "

4.

But grim Jack Hart, with a sneer,
  Would mutter, " Master !
If Freedom means to appear,
I think she might step *here*
  A little faster ! "
Then, 'twas fine to see Tom flame,
  And argue, and prove, and preach,
Till Jack was silent for shame,—
Or a fit of coughing came
  O' sudden, to spoil Tom's speech.

Ah! Tom had the eyes to see
    When the tyrants would be sped :
"She's coming! she's coming!" said he ;
"Courage, boys! wait and see !
    Freedom's ahead ! "

5.

But Tom was little and weak,
    The hard hours shook him ;
Hollower grew his cheek,
And when he began to speak
    The coughing took him.
And at last the cheery sound
    Of his voice among us ceased,
And we made a purse, all round,
    That he mightn't starve, at least.
His pain was awful to see,
    Yet there, on his poor sick-bed,
"She's coming, in spite of me !
Courage, and wait !" cried he ;
    " *Freedom's* ahead ! "

6.

A little before he died,
    To see his passion !
" Bring me a Paper ! " he cried,
And then to study it tried,
    In his old sharp fashion ;
And, with eyeballs glittering,
    His look on me he bent,
And said that savage thing
    Of the Lords o' the Parliament.
Then, dying, smiling on me,
    " What matter if *one* be dead ?
She's coming at last ! " said he ;
    " Courage, boy! wait and see ;
        Freedom's ahead ! "

7.

Ay, now Tom Dunstan's cold,
  All life seems duller ;
There's a blight on young and old,
And our talk has lost the bold
  Red-republican colour.
But we see a figure gray,
  And we hear a voice of death,
And the tallow burns all day,
And we stitch and stitch away
  In the thick smoke of our breath ;
Ay, while in the dark sit we,
  Tom seems to call from the dead—
"She's coming! she's coming!" says he;
" Courage, boys! wait and see!
  Freedom's ahead ! "

How long, O Lord ! how long
  Must Thy Handmaid linger
She who shall right the wrong,
Make the poor sufferer strong ?
  Sweet morrow, bring her !
Hasten her over the sea,
  O Lord! ere Hope be fled !
Send her to make men free ! . . .
O Slave, pray still on thy knee,
  " FREEDOM's *ahead !* "

L'ENVOI TO "BUCHANAN BALLADS."

I do not sing for Maidens. They are
roses
Blowing along the pathway I pursue :
No sweeter things the wondrous world
discloses,
And they are tender as the morning
dew.
Blessed be maids and children : day
and night
Their holy scent is with me as I write.

I do not sing for Schoolboys or School-
men.
To give them ease I have no languid
theme,
When, weary with the wear of book
and pen,
They seek their trim poetic Aca-
deme ;
Nor can I sing them amorous ditties,
bred
Of too much Ovid on an empty head.

I do not sing aloud in measured tone
Of those fair paths the easy-soul'd
pursue :
Nor do I sing for Lazarus alone,
I sing for Dives, and the Devil too.
Ah! would the feeble songs I sing
might swell
As high as Heaven, and as deep as
Hell !

I sing of the stain'd outcast at Love's
feet,—
Love with his wild eyes on the evening light ;
I sing of sad lives trampled down like
wheat
Under the heel of Lust, in Love's
despite ;

I glean behind those wretched shape
ye see
In the cold harvest-fields of Infamy.

I sing of death-beds (let no man re-
joice
Till that last piteous touch of all is
given!) ;
I sing of Death and Life with equal
voice,
Heaven watching Hell, and Hell
illumed by Heaven.
I have gone deep, far down the in-
fernal stair—
And seen the heirs of Heaven arising
there !

I sing of Hope, that all the lost may
hear ;
I sing of Light, that all may feel its
ray ;
I sing of Souls, that no one Soul may
fear ;
I sing of God, that some perchance
may pray.
Angels in hosts have praised Him
loud and long,
But Man's shall be the last triumphal
Song.

Oh, hush a space the sounds of voices
light
Mix'd to the music of a lover's lute.
Stranger than dream, so luminously
bright
Eyes shall be dazzled and the mouth
be mute,
Man shall arise, Lord of all things that
be,
Last of the gods, and Heir of all things
free !